Immunising the Children of the World

Immunising the Children of the World

Ralph H. Henderson

Orient BlackSwan

IMMUNISING THE CHILDREN OF THE WORLD

ORIENT BLACKSWAN PRIVATE LIMITED

Registered Office
3-6-752 Himayatnagar, Hyderabad 500 029 (Telangana), India
e-mail: centraloffice@orientblackswan.com

Other Offices
Bengaluru, Bhopal, Chennai, Ernakulam,
Guwahati, Hyderabad, Jaipur, Kolkata,
Lucknow, Mumbai, New Delhi, Noida, Patna, Vijayawada

First published by Orient Blackswan Private Limited 2016

ISBN 978 81 250 6419 0

Typeset by
Le Studio Graphique, Gurgaon 122 001
in Calisto MT 10/12

Printed at
Yash Printographics
Noida

023686

08082016

Published by
Orient Blackswan Private Limited
1/24 Asaf Ali Road
New Delhi 110 002
e-mail: delhi@orientblackswan.com

Contents

Figures and Box

Figures

Box

Preface

Celebration! The UNICEF video for the 1990 World Summit for Children exclaimed: 'We have done the impossible! But our task has just begun.' Some 80 per cent of the world's children were now being immunised.[1] Nobody could have imagined such progress could occur so quickly. It was a triumph, despite coverage in the least developed countries being only 55 per cent, our unfinished task.

Just 16 years previously, barely 5 per cent of children in the developing world were receiving any immunisations and most of those were of doubtful quality. That dismal statistic refers to 1974, the year the World Health Assembly established the Expanded Program on Immunization (EPI). But by 1976, the programme had almost collapsed! The director-general saved it, changing the EPI coordinator and providing more adequate resources. The EPI then quickly grew to train national staff in management, to lead the development of new products to keep vaccines cold and injections safe, and to identify and promote 'best practices' for immunisation services in developing countries.

When he became UNICEF executive director in 1980, Jim (James P.) Grant was sceptical about supporting the EPI. But he soon changed his mind. His personal advocacy and his commitment of UNICEF's financial resources and national staff were the major factors in allowing national programmes to accelerate so fast. He would not, nor could not, however, have done this without the foundations laid by World Health Organization's (WHO's) EPI.

FIGURE P1: 'Immunize and Protect Your Child'. Poster Issued for World Health Day, 1977

Source: Reproduced with permission from the World Health Organization, Geneva.

Although UNICEF has received justified credit for its role in supporting immunisation, I think WHO has not. I write this account mainly to tell our story. It is based on my experience serving with the EPI as programme manager and then director from 1977 to 1989, and then as WHO assistant director-general from 1990 to 1999. Our story is a bit like a Bismarck sausage—the ingredients were not always pretty but the outcome was excellent. Please enjoy!

Notes

1. WHO/UNICEF (see 'immunization; global and regional data and statistics' at http://www.who.int/immunization/monitoring_surveillance/data/regions/en/). Over the past decades, WHO and UNICEF have continued their joint efforts to improve data on immunisation coverage. The separation of data between all and least developed countries was not available early on. All data in the charts reflects the WHO/UNICEF revision of July 2012. DPT is used as the indicator vaccine. The estimate for DPT-3 in 1990 is 75 per cent.

Part 1

Learning the Ropes

1

The Adventures Begin!

I'm goin' down the road feelin' bad...

Woody Guthrie

West Africa: First Contact

It was 3 AM on Sunday, 23 October 1965. I was in bed in Bobo-Dioulasso (Burkina Faso) and I was, indeed, 'feelin' bad'. Tom Mack, my Centers for Disease Control and Prevention (CDC) companion, was soundly asleep in the adjoining bed. After a violent bout of diarrhoea and vomiting, I got back to bed to recover. A few short hours later, we introduced ourselves to Dr Pierre Richet, the secretary-general of the French colonial organisation that coordinated public health programmes in eight Francophone countries of West Africa.[1] I had been assigned as technical advisor to make myself useful to the measles immunisation programmes that the United States Agency for International Development (USAID) had started funding in these countries the year before. Tom soon left to take up an assignment in East Pakistan (now Bangladesh) that had been suspended due to civil war.

USAID had got into the measles business largely, if not entirely, for political reasons. The United States (US) had the only licensed measles vaccine at that time and studies in Upper Volta (now Burkina Faso) by the US National Institutes of Health (NIH) showed it worked (Meyer et al. 1964). Moreover, a follow-on mass campaign had succeeded in virtually eliminating the disease and the effort was wildly popular. The US had a diplomatic coup in hand! The French had nothing to match it. Making diplomatic inroads on colonial turf in Africa had been a US goal since the end of World War II (WWII).

USAID provided the measles vaccine, jet injectors, and supplies and equipment including 'crew cab' Dodge trucks. The latter would prove to be long-lasting workhorses, although not enough spare parts had been provided and none were available locally. In addition, they guzzled gasoline that the countries themselves had to supply. These were not the only problems.

Larry Altman, now a respected *New York Times* journalist, had preceded me in the immunisation programme to West Africa. His performance had not endeared him to the higher echelons at USAID. He had informed Washington that the refrigerators on the Dodges were not able to overcome the blazing Sahel heat, putting the measles vaccine at risk. They suggested the trucks be parked under trees. He cabled back requesting trees. To add to existing challenges, a regrettable oversight in the design of the trucks placed the open flame of the propane refrigerators close to the jerry cans filled with spare gasoline. Fortunately, there were no human casualties from the resulting explosions.

Larry gave me a thorough briefing on what to pack and what to expect. In contrast, the sum total of the briefing I received from USAID was 'Keep the image clean', which was good enough as it turned out.

Barely four months previously, in July 1965, I had reported for duty to the CDC in Atlanta as a brand new Epidemic Intelligence Service (EIS) Officer. I was leaving the Harvard Services of the Boston City Hospital after an internship and first-year residency in internal medicine. I completed the traditionally brief two-month training at CDC under the watchful eye of Dr Alex Langmuir, founder of the EIS and legendary character and epidemiologist. Then I joined the smallpox unit directed by Dr D. A. Henderson (no relation, henceforth DA) and this led to my West African assignment. The following year (1966), DA would go to the World Health Organization (WHO) to direct the global programme of smallpox eradication.

I spent some six months travelling the OCCGE countries learning about the basic logistics and daily travails of the mobile teams delivering immunisation services. On leaving the US, I had been issued a thick booklet of 'GTRs' or Government Travel

Requests. These were basically blank cheques allowing me to buy airline tickets (or other transport) as I wished, saving all concerned a lot of trouble in giving me a new authorisation when flights were changed or cancelled, as they frequently were.

My official duties were to serve as the liaison with USAID country offices and, with them, to try to solve problems with the supplies and equipment being sent from Washington. So we had to make emergency requests for 'points' needed for the electric-powered jet injectors, which were unavailable in the local markets. And we had to request more diluent for the measles vaccine, for which bottled Evian water was being substituted in some countries.

I saw and learned a lot about what could, and did, go wrong! For example, the jet injectors often needed cleaning and it was onerous to boil the parts before reassembling them, especially as crowds waited. So that step was frequently omitted. Not so easy to remedy. And some of the immunisation teams kept the measles vaccine diluent on top of their trucks and added it hot to the heat-sensitive vaccine kept in the refrigerators. That was more easily corrected. Despite these and other problems, we received no reports of adverse reactions and the programme was highly popular, with large crowds being the norm.

My chief mentors were the dynamic and young French Médecin Militaires who served as the principal advisors to the ministries of health in these countries. They were extraordinarily generous with their time and patience, especially needed as, at least initially, I had only a smattering of French.

My very first introduction to a 'Chef des Grandes Endémies' (Director of the Major Endemic Diseases) did not go well, however. We met soon after my arrival in Ouagadougou, capital of Upper Volta. He was Hubert Sansarricq. He was not cordial. He was furious. He told me in terms even I could understand that our Dodges had consumed his entire annual gasoline budget. It was ironic that we would both join WHO headquarters and that I would later, as assistant director-general, become his supervisor. I do not recall either of us acknowledging we had known each other in Africa.

As I moved up the bureaucratic ladder in later years, I realised how much information gets lost, or actively suppressed, in that ladder. When I had no status I saw activities as they were habitually performed, warts and all. In the presence of higher authority, those warts are hidden. But even under such circumstances, seeing for yourself is important. As a colleague said: 'You don't know if you don't go.'

In January 1966, midway in my assignment, the Smallpox Eradication/Measles Control Program of West and Central Africa emerged from DA's negotiations with USAID. USAID wanted a measles immunisation programme, extending its efforts in French West Africa. But USAID needed technical help from the CDC. DA cared little about measles, but a lot about smallpox eradication. So the bargain for the new programme including both diseases was struck. CDC established a regional office in Lagos, Nigeria, and, in light of my vast experience (months!) and while I was still travelling in West Africa, DA designated me its deputy chief and epidemiologist. Talk about being in the right place at the right time! I returned to CDC in March 1966 and Ilze Sarma and I married that May.

An Interlude for Ilze

Why Ilze? Ilze has counted throughout my career, helping with surveys, attending meetings, hosting social events, and acting as my administrative assistant. Her daily journal, started in Africa and still maintained, has been a source for this account. I could not guess when we met, however, what adventures she had had.

Ilze was born in Riga, Latvia, in 1933. During WWII, the Germans had to cede to the Russians and withdraw from Latvia. In October 1944, they took her surgeon-father, a valuable asset, with them. Fortunately, they took the rest of the family (mother, baby sister Maija, and 11-year-old Ilze) with them too. By May 1945, Germany had surrendered and the family became displaced persons, remaining in American displaced persons (DP) camps until 1949. In that year, Soviet deportations of Latvian citizens to Siberia ended their dreams of going home and they accepted the offer of an American physician, made in 1945, to co-sponsor them in the US.

The family arrived in Clewiston, Florida, in October 1949, perspiring in their heavy winter clothes. They found their sponsor had become addicted to narcotics and was in no shape to help with support. His girlfriend wanted to get rid of the Sarma family at the earliest. To this end, she appealed to Jack Bell, a columnist at the *Miami Herald*, who was known for his general good works.

Bell moved the family to Miami and arranged for Dr Sarma to get a job in the hospital central sterile devices department, sterilising instruments, while Ilze's mother worked three jobs housecleaning (and earned more than her husband). Ilze, 16, joined the Bell family, taking care of their two daughters as an *au pair*. Within a year or so the family moved to Milledgeville, Georgia, where her father became a 'psychiatrist' (no special accreditation required) at what was deemed the nation's largest mental hospital. Ilze graduated from Peabody High School there and went on to the University of Georgia to become a pharmacist. She moved to Atlanta to work at the Emory University Hospital.

We met in July 1965, just after my arrival at CDC. Another CDC recruit and I went looking for an apartment. A manager at one complex said he had something nice next to three single young women. We did not hesitate! Ilze and I soon became acquainted. I soon left, however, to go on a prearranged sailing date in Maine with a girlfriend from medical school. In preparation, I bought a Public Health Service uniform so I could fly half fare. Ilze obliged by sewing gold stripes on it. (I looked ridiculous: the lady at the airline counter asked, 'Are you a student, Lt. Commander?')

Shortly after getting back from sailing, I was sent off to West Africa for six months. Ilze and I parted without any commitments, yet I think we had no doubts. Ilze met me at the Atlanta airport on my return in March 1966 and we married that May. I was kept busy at CDC from March through September in helping to train the next class of EIS officers. Ilze and I also had training along with the 40-some professionals and their families who would be our West African colleagues. This included a vehicle maintenance course for the professionals (the course for us physicians was dumbed down from that given to the 'operations officers') and an intensive French course for the professionals and family dealing with the Francophone countries.

We departed for Lagos in October 1966. It was not without incident! We were to live out of our suitcases until our airfreight arrived and I had firm ideas, based on my previous months of wandering, of what was and was not needed. Ilze stood by, horrified, as I went through her carefully packed suitcase throwing out item after item I considered non-essential. Of course she also knew a thing or two about living under constrained circumstances and it is a tribute to her tolerance that she only reinstated a few items. It was not my best moment!

More Adventures

At the CDC Regional Office in Lagos for the smallpox programme, in addition to putting out a newsletter that we sent to our colleagues in the various countries, I continued my previous role as troubleshooter. Problems now included smoothing relationships between the USAID country officers—kings in their own fiefdoms—and our country staff who were serving a regional project and had responsibilities outside of their home-base countries. And I also tried to help in soothing the irritations of the ministries of health over receiving Dodge trucks and the problems of spare parts and high gasoline consumption.

Ilze came with me to Abidjan, Côte d'Ivoire, in November 1966 to attend a meeting. Her journal entry for 6 November simply says 'Adzopé!' That was sufficient code. We had been taken by bus to visit a famous leper colony there. The village had prepared for us, festooning the main street with large banners. As the bus sped through, it took banner after banner with it! We arrived to tour the colony, but our driver decided we had better return by another route.

We left Africa for a brief interlude in the spring of 1967 when I was sent to India with two CDC colleagues. A large smallpox epidemic there was resulting in cases being imported to Europe, each raising public alarm and being costly to manage. The Government of India was under pressure to accept outside help. That was us: three young and enthusiastic epidemiologists and a few jet injectors ready to go to work immediately.

It was not to be. Not long after our arrival, our exasperated Ministry of Health supervisor put the problem in a nutshell by asking us: 'What do you say to a friend who, as a gesture of friendship, gives you an elephant?' The ministry could not conceive how to make use of us! Fortunately, the monsoon came, the epidemic subsided, and we left after a frustrating four weeks of accomplishing little, although discovering problems galore with the Indian programme that were neither acknowledged nor remedied.

While we were in India, however, Eastern Nigeria declared independence, resulting in the Biafran War. The US embassy decreed that dependents then out of the country could not return. Ilze was marooned. But I was able to negotiate with the CDC to become an itinerant troubleshooter. Our staff in the various countries faced both technical and political problems and I was able to help with both. We spent the next few months in travel status visiting Dahomey (now Benin), Togo, Ghana, Mali, Côte d'Ivoire, Upper Volta and Niger. I discuss ahead the smallpox we encountered in the first two.

In Dahomey, we noticed a woman in the market with a large pustule in the middle of her forehead. We suspected this was the result of variolation: applying actual smallpox (variola) virus to the skin as a protective measure. (Samples I sent to CDC later confirmed these suspicions.) We knew that variolation was usually performed by traditional healers when there was smallpox. So we traced the woman back to her village of Toffo-Gâre and conducted a detailed study of this smallpox outbreak to show how the disease spread from family to family (Henderson and Yekpe 1969). There were 28 cases in this village of 300, occurring over a period of more than three months. The map (Figure 1.1) is a copy of Ilze's original drawing and was reproduced in the article cited above. It added to the mounting evidence that, contrary to the general belief at the time, smallpox transmission most often requires close contact.

In Togo we helped convince the Ministry of Health to stop trying to enforce a generalised 'cordon sanitaire' to isolate a smallpox epidemic that was occurring in a WHO demonstration zone (some demonstration!). They switched instead to controlling contact with infected patients and to identifying and vaccinating all known contacts, a new strategy that we were using that had been devised in Eastern Nigeria by one of our staff, Bill (William H.) Foege (more on this later). That ended the outbreak.

We returned to our home in Lagos later that year (1967) and I had another job change: the CDC HQ staff asked me to carry out a number of programme assessments that had been requested by USAID. That was no small job! It included estimating the coverage with measles and smallpox (vaccinia) vaccines. What I could not imagine at the time was that the simplified coverage survey method I adapted (discussed later) would blossom to become perhaps the most frequently used in the world. Between June 1968 and January 1969, I dutifully completed assessments of three areas in Nigeria and a national assessment of Niger, assembling teams from our regional office and country staff to help.

FIGURE 1.1: Copy of Ilze's Hand-drawn Map of Toffo Gare

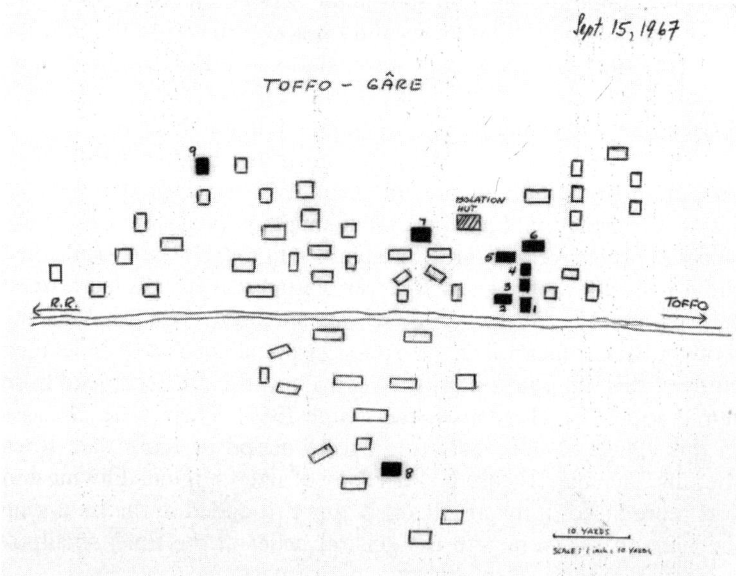

Note: Black rectangles indicate houses in which smallpox cases occurred and are numbered in the order of the dates of the first occurrence of a case in that household.

Source: R. H. Henderson and M. Yekpe, 'Smallpox Transmission in Southern Dahomey: A Study of a Village Outbreak', *American Journal of Epidemiology* 90, 1 November 1969. Permission received through Copyright Clearance Center, Inc.

For the surveys, each team had a list of randomly selected areas or villages to visit. In each, they interviewed residents and collected information on their age, sex, vaccination status, and other items. They marked boxes printed on a specially designed 'McBee^{R}' card to record the information for each person. Each evening the team leader used a paper punch to cut a notch in the edge of the card corresponding to each box that had been checked (Figure 1.2).

I did the final analysis myself. At the end of these surveys I had analysed some 15,000 cards. This meant taking a stack and running a knitting needle through a specific hole and shaking until all cards notched at that spot dropped out. If I skewered hole number 3, the cards for everyone aged 15–44 years dropped out. If I took those

FIGURE 1.2: McBee[R] Card

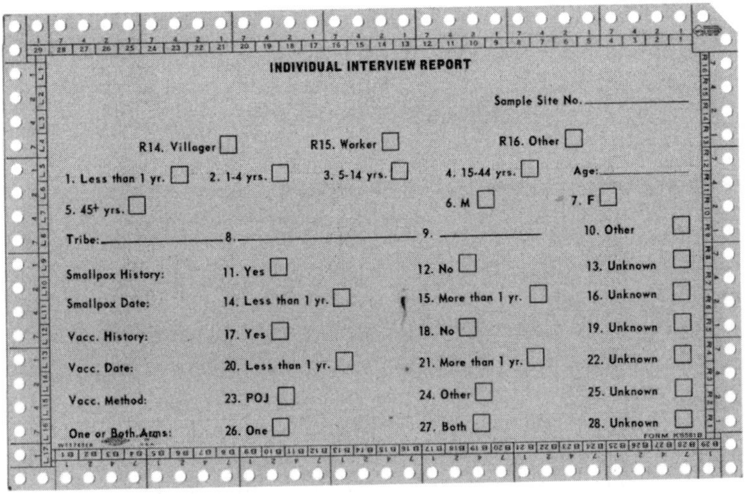
INDIVIDUAL INTERVIEW REPORT

Sample Site No. ______

R14. Villager ☐ R15. Worker ☐ R16. Other ☐

1. Less than 1 yr. ☐ 2. 1-4 yrs. ☐ 3. 5-14 yrs. ☐ 4. 15-44 yrs. ☐ Age: ______

5. 45+ yrs. ☐ 6. M ☐ 7. F ☐

Tribe: ______ 8. ______ 9. ______ 10. Other ☐

Smallpox History: 11. Yes ☐ 12. No ☐ 13. Unknown ☐

Smallpox Date: 14. Less than 1 yr. ☐ 15. More than 1 yr. ☐ 16. Unknown ☐

Vacc. History: 17. Yes ☐ 18. No ☐ 19. Unknown ☐

Vacc. Date: 20. Less than 1 yr. ☐ 21. More than 1 yr. ☐ 22. Unknown ☐

Vacc. Method: 23. POJ ☐ 24. Other ☐ 25. Unknown ☐

One or Both Arms: 26. One ☐ 27. Both ☐ 28. Unknown ☐

cards and skewered hole number 6, I got the cards for all males of that age. That was tedious, to say the least!

Ilze and I headed teams in northern and western Nigeria and a team in Niger. We had many good and some bad adventures with miles of dusty or muddy tracks and roads, vehicles stuck and disabled, and marvellous journeys by horseback and dugout canoe to reach selected villages. We returned tired and dirty one memorable evening to a rest house bungalow in a malaria programme compound in northern Nigeria. We were desperate for a shower, but it was the dry season and there was no rain, hence no water.

I was prepared, however! I had taken water with us. I hoisted a jerry can to the shelf above the bathtub and put in a hose. Naked, we gathered underneath. I sucked on the tubing to start the siphon. I spit out a mouthful of water. Nothing further happened. After repeated sucking failures I was stumped. Ilze said, 'Shorten the hose.' Silly woman! I knew a thing or two about siphons and that had nothing to do with it. So I sucked some more. And Ilze said, 'Shorten the hose', again. Furious and frustrated, I cut the hose. And water flowed!

Ilze had a far better intuitive understanding of the situation than I did. I had cursed evil spirits, but it was simply a case of the jerry being pretty low and the hose with a long loop. The friction in the hose overcame the gravity pull of the siphon. This experience was one of many that have worked wonders for my humility centre and have certainly tested Ilze's patience.

Domestic Interlude

Masters degrees and social diseases

In early 1967, Bill Foege, a former EIS officer, had been serving as a Lutheran missionary in Eastern Nigeria when CDC persuaded him to join the smallpox/measles programme there. He had been faced with a smallpox epidemic and did not have enough vaccine to conduct a mass vaccination campaign, the approach then in general use throughout the world. So he conserved the vaccine by locating cases and identifying and vaccinating their close contacts. (Vaccination within a week or so prevents exposed persons from becoming ill and infecting others.) Even though coverage in the general population was low, this selective vaccination worked spectacularly. This 'surveillance and containment' strategy was applied in West Africa and smallpox quickly disappeared. It became the strategy for WHO's Global Smallpox Eradication Program. Foege describes its specific application in India in his book, *Fire Next Door* (Foege 2011).

By the end of 1968, smallpox was about to vanish; it was time for me to move on. I wrote to Dr David Sencer, CDC director, requesting a Public Health Service Career Development grant, allowing me to receive an additional two years of formal training. He approved my application and Ilze and I arrived in Boston in the fall of 1969. I received my Harvard Master of Public Health in the spring of 1970. For my second year, I wanted to enter the John F. Kennedy School of Government's Master of Public Policy programme. It was exactly what I was looking for. But at age 31 they thought I was too old. They wanted fresh college or medical or law school graduates. I had to work hard to convince them I was worth their investment. I entered in the fall of 1970. Not only did I survive one of the hardest, and most productive, academic years of my career, I was even elected class president! (Old guys sometimes prevail!)

The Kennedy School training ended in the fall of 1971 and Sencer gave me free reign to look for work anywhere within the Public Health Service. This was generous of him, as the training was really intended as preparation for a career in high-level policymaking, not for a technical position in an agency such as the CDC, and I was certainly interested in looking around. I went to Washington, D.C. for a few days to look at options. But it all looked too bureaucratic to me. Sencer promised that if I returned to the CDC he would find me a responsible position as soon as one materialised.

I did just that and so did he. In 1972, after spending time in his Program Performance and Evaluation Office (that I detested), he appointed me assistant chief of the Venereal Disease Control Division (henceforth VD Division). Within a few months, the chief was promoted and I replaced him. I had some difficulties in making the transition from smallpox. In my earlier position I seemed to have known everyone and done everything. But the VD Division had close to 60 staff at the CDC, another 500 or so federal staff in the United States, and 1,500 or more state or local employees. In addition, I was no VD expert; I knew nothing and nobody. Yet I learned to manage.

Happily, the VD staff welcomed me warmly, and along with my supervisors provided me mentoring. I was able to help lead the division through its transition from focusing narrowly on syphilis to encompassing gonorrhoea as well (then an epidemic). The medical staff changed from being dermatologists to infectious disease specialists and epidemiologists. The incidence of gonorrhoea began to decline and we were well positioned to take on the challenge of other sexually transmitted diseases, although hardly imagining the challenges ahead presented by HIV/AIDS!

It was Sencer, again, who gave me a new assignment. CDC had seconded DA to WHO's smallpox eradication programme in 1966, and he had been expected to take over the Expanded Program on Immunization (EPI) once smallpox was eradicated. But he had unexpectedly decided to leave to become Dean of the Johns Hopkins School of Hygiene and Public Health.

At the time, the EPI was struggling, with its temporary management under criticism for its lack of progress (discussed later). The CDC wanted to send an EPI manager as a replacement for DA. So in the fall of 1976, Sencer called me at home one evening to ask if I was interested.[2] By then the VD Division was in good shape and my deputy was more than able to replace me. Ilze and I jumped at the chance.

NOTES

1. The formal name of the organisation is Organisation de Coordination et de Coopération pour la lutte contre les Grandes Endémies (OCCGE). At the time, it covered (from west to east) Mauritania, Senegal, Mali, Upper Volta (now Burkina Faso), Côte d'Ivoire, Togo, Dahomey (now Benin), and Niger. It was at that time being 'Africanised', but with negligible impact.

2. Bill Foege would likely have been chosen except that he and his family had only recently returned from several brutally difficult smallpox years in India and he was not ready for another extended international assignment.

Part 2

The EPI

2

The Origins of the Expanded Programme on Immunisation (EPI)

Standing on the Shoulders of Giants

It was May 1974. Smallpox was close to eradication and the time was ripe for using that success to launch a broad childhood immunisation initiative. The World Health Assembly (WHA), the governing body of the World Health Organization (WHO), established the Expanded Program on Immunization (EPI) (Resolution WHA27.57).

Immunisation services in developing countries at that time were appalling. No international information system providing coverage estimates existed, but information from vaccine manufacturers suggested that coverage in developing countries could not be above 5 per cent. Millions of children died each year from vaccine-preventable diseases, including whooping cough (pertussis), measles, poliomyelitis, and neonatal tetanus. National immunisation schedules, where they could be found, were most often relics of the policies of colonial days. Too often, the vaccines were impotent and the injections were not safe (more on this later). Potency and safety were better in the Americas, but here the emphasis was on immunising school-age children. This was too late for diseases that most often struck before two years of age.

The EPI was to assist Member States in developing suitable immunisation programmes, in assuring the availability of good quality vaccines at reasonable cost, and in mobilising support for national programmes and for research and development. The programme was meant to 'expand' both coverage and the number of vaccines given to children in the first two years of life. Besides smallpox, these included BCG (used against tuberculosis), DPT (diphtheria, pertussis and tetanus), measles and oral polio (OPV) vaccines. Tetanus Toxoid was also to be administered to pregnant women to prevent neonatal tetanus. Although the freeze-dried smallpox vaccine was extremely stable, all the others needed some degree of heat protection, the most sensitive being the measles and polio vaccines.

The introduction of these latter two vaccines was a major step for immunisation services in developing countries. Studies in West Africa in the 1960s had confirmed the lethality of measles, already too apparent to residents who sometimes stampeded to receive the vaccine. Yet health authorities in much of Asia did not consider measles a problem despite studies showing otherwise (Dave 1983), and this same attitude persisted in much of Europe into the 1980s.

Polio was dreaded in industrialised countries, with epidemics beginning to appear in Europe and then the United States (US) in the late 1800s. The paralysis of Franklin Delano Roosevelt at age 29 in the year 1921 was a prelude to increasingly severe epidemics in the US in the 1940s. Improving living conditions delayed children being exposed, and this delay increased the risk of paralysis, in part because of ebbing maternal antibodies. In developing countries, children were infected soon after birth, and it was widely assumed they suffered little consequence.

Not so! In Ghana, in the early 1970s, a comprehensive rural health and family planning programme known as the DANFA project (Ofosu-Amaah, et al. 1977) documented that poliomyelitis was, in fact, a major problem. In 1977, they published two papers in the *British Medical Journal* (ibid.; Nicholas, et al. 1977) showing that lameness rates from poliomyelitis were comparable to those suffered in the US and Europe during the years of severe epidemics. And they showed that there was a high mortality rate among young children from polio, hidden among the many other causes of death in such environments.

The EPI benefitted from technical work done in the preceding decade on the safety and efficacy of simultaneously administering various combinations of vaccines. So, for example, studies were done to show that the DPT vaccine could be given at the same time as the oral polio vaccine. They confirmed that the measles vaccine could be given with both DPT and polio, but should not be given before nine months because maternal antibodies would interfere. Much of this work had been conducted by the Centers for Disease Control and Prevention (CDC) staff during the smallpox/measles programme in West Africa. The EPI would apply these results and would also profit from the experience with outreach services and applied epidemiology gained by the many national and international smallpox staff that would soon join.

The EPI logo that was designed (see Figure 2.1) was a huge success. It is a stylised figure of a mother embracing a child whose head and body form an 'i'. It quickly spread beyond WHO to become an internationally recognised symbol of high quality, appearing on commercial cold chain products and used within national immunisation programmes with our full support and blessing. A later WHO HQ supervisor tried, for reasons best known to him, to discard it, but failed. It remains a thrill to see it still displayed in health centres around the world.

FIGURE 2.1: The EPI Logo,[1] First Used in the Poster for World Health Day 1974

Source: Reproduced with the permission of the World Health Organization, Geneva, 12 November 2014.

A LITTLE HELP FROM OUR FRIENDS

WHO had few resources to invest in this new initiative (the EPI); it was only help from the outside that permitted any progress to be made at all.

The Danish International Development Agency (DANIDA), a strong supporter of the smallpox programme, had made a contribution of some $160,000. It supported the services of consultants and allowed WHO to convene several regional meetings between 1974 and 1977 to promote the programme. In addition, the UK Overseas Development Agency (ODA) supported John Lloyd, an architect, who provided cold chain and logistics consultancies starting in 1976.[2]

The Swedish International Development Agency (SIDA), another strong smallpox programme supporter, financed studies comparing the coverage and costs of delivering immunisation services through mobile teams with delivery using existing health facilities. They confirmed that the mobile teams achieved higher immunisation coverage. But the research was a bit unfair to the health centres. Ghana had a long tradition of excellent mobile teams who had been given responsibility for providing immunisation. The mobile teams provided services to areas not within the reach of health centres. They had a separate staff and separate organisation. By tradition, the teams gave immunisations, as they reached far more people than the health centres. The nurses just did not see this as their responsibility. Even if the nurses had welcomed this new responsibility, there were not enough centres to reach the populations in need.

SIDA also provided funds to the Swedish National Microbiology Laboratory for the development and testing of a cold box. This was produced by the laboratory using the design that John Lloyd and the laboratory director, Holger Lundbeck, developed. It was the first long-life cold box to be designed specifically for vaccines. It was the model for many successors that became widely produced both for sale internationally and within national programmes.[3]

The SIDA studies on coverage also tested the cold chain. The young WHO medical officer assigned to support and monitor them was Serguei Litvinov from the erstwhile Union of Soviet Socialist Republics (USSR). Serguei (who will resurface later as my supervising assistant director-general) was doing a heroic job during a period of deep recession in an environment of runaway inflation, fuel shortages and unmotivated staff. He took scrupulous care of the cold chain using the cold boxes mentioned above. The vaccine samples returned from the field for titration in Sweden were still fully potent.

And yet the sero-conversion rates for polio, especially type 3, were abysmal. We behaved badly at headquarters, telling ourselves despite contrary evidence that this was a cold chain problem. It took the warnings of Joseph L. Melnick, one of polio's pioneering greats, to make us admit that something else was wrong. When children are exposed to poor sanitary conditions, they become heavily exposed to the 'enteroviruses' that live in human intestines, poliovirus among them. These interfere with the polio virus contained in the vaccine. Challenges in trying to solve this problem remain.[4]

Notes

1. The logo and poster were designed by Peter Davies. He was a British citizen employed by the World Health Organization (WHO) as a freelance art director before becoming a public information officer and designing layouts for the WHO journal *World Health: The Magazine of the World Health Organization*. The logo echoed the theme of a sculpture by artist Sava Sandić that was accepted by WHO in 1966 from the government of Yugoslavia (in Belgrade at the time, now Serbia). This was when any member state could offer gifts to furbish/decorate the then new WHO building.

2. J. Lloyd, in an email dated 20 February 2013.

3. But they were almost too good! One unexpected problem was the accidental freezing of liquid bacterial vaccines such as DPT and tetanus. They could be inactivated by freezing and needed to be well-insulated from the ice packs.

4. See Melnick (1982). We finally admitted this problem to ourselves in the mid-1980s. Ciro de Quadros, the Pan American Health Organization (PAHO) EPI coordinator, convinced Wyeth, our major Oral Polio Vaccine (OPV) supplier, to increase the type 3 titer in our vaccines by, I think, 0.3 log from 5.5 to 5.8. This was deemed only a token change and, in fact, no impact was observed. The problem persists to this day in environments that are swamped with other enteroviruses that compete with the three polio vaccine strains. The first approach was to advocate giving additional doses that, of course, causes its own problems. Later, when type 2 wild virus had been eliminated, a vaccine using only types 1 and 3 was introduced that does improve the 'take' rates, although multiple doses are still needed. In developing countries at continuing risk of polio, the debate continues on introducing the Salk killed vaccine either alone or in combination with the Sabin live vaccine.

3

Introduction to the World Health Organization (WHO)

WHO knows everything and does nothing; UNICEF knows nothing and does everything; the World Bank knows everything and does everything and UNDP knows nothing and does nothing.

(Personal communication from a highly placed friend at WHO)

The EPI was first managed mainly by staff on loan. Frank Schofield, the acting programme coordinator, came from the Health Manpower Division. He was assisted by Fakhry Assaad from the Communicable Disease Division. The only full-time staff consisted of a medical officer, Ko (Jacobus) Keja, and a secretary, Coby Sikkens.

Frank had an excellent reputation from his work on training health staff while working for the British colonial medical services in Kenya. But he did not inspire confidence as EPI coordinator and was being subjected to loud, withering and continuous criticism from Dr D. A. Henderson.

Frank was committed to health services development. He was of the firm view that immunisation services should expand only at the rate of the health services as a whole. Anathema to DA! Smallpox eradication had succeeded only because it reached beyond the established services and childhood immunisation should do the same, building infrastructure as it went. Things were bad enough that by 1976, consideration was being given to eliminating the Expanded

Program on Immunization (EPI), especially since DA, having decided to leave for Johns Hopkins, would not be taking it over.

It was in November 1976 that I had agreed to Dr Sencer's proposal to go to the World Health Organization (WHO) and I was there the next month to interview with director-general Halfdan Mahler and his senior staff. I am not sure he was thrilled by the prospect, but the Centers for Disease Control and Prevention (CDC) and the WHO had good relations, and the fact that the United States (US) contributed a quarter of WHO's regular budget certainly did no harm.[1] DA had not yet departed and took time in helping me to prepare. It was very good that he did.

The smallpox unit at WHO headquarters had been run with four medical officers, one administrative officer, one technical officer, and four secretaries. These were regular budget posts, meaning that the funding was pretty much ensured so long as the programme existed. But regular budget positions are very expensive as they include, in addition to the salary of the staff member, cost of living adjustments, retirement benefits, school support for children, and health insurance for the entire family. They were, and are, extremely hard to come by!

DA thought the EPI needed a larger number. So we agreed I would push for 16 positions. In our meeting, however, after I had proposed 16, Dr Mahler stated that the maximum would be 10, the size of the former smallpox unit, and indicated that our meeting was over. This was a very difficult moment for me! I was still on trial. But I was convinced that DA was correct in insisting on a critical mass of core staff and I hesitantly said that I did not think I could direct this programme with the number proposed. The EPI's feeble outreach to the WHO Regional Offices and countries and the negligible training efforts done so far would not suffice!

Dr Joe Cohen, Mahler's principal advisor, then suggested allocating 12 full-time positions and providing sufficient additional regular budget funds to permit the hiring of up to four additional short-term staff per year. (They are cheaper. They receive a salary and per diem allowance, but no other benefits.) He argued that this would provide more staffing flexibility than having the same number of full-time staff. This seemed a reasonable compromise and I agreed.

To my great relief, Dr Mahler accepted and, in doing so, also accepted me. This was a big risk for him. I was 40 years old (considered very young to become a director at WHO) and had only my West African experience for international credentials. I returned to Atlanta but not before renting an apartment and buying a car. By March 1977, Ilze and I were on site. These were heady days!

The studies and cold chain development work that the Swedish International Development Cooperation Agency (SIDA) had supported in Ghana were part of the legacy I inherited, which allowed us to get going quickly. The EPI was already scheduled to report to the World Health Assembly (WHA) that May. I scrambled with Ko to prepare it. We summarised the progress to date (not so very much!) and proposed that the EPI objectives include reducing morbidity and mortality by providing immunisation to every child in the world by 1990. That was ambitious (Figure 3.1)![2] The WHA endorsed the report in full (Resolution WHA30.53).

FIGURE 3.1: Immunisation Coverage Estimate for Developing Countries, 1974, and 1990 EPI Goal

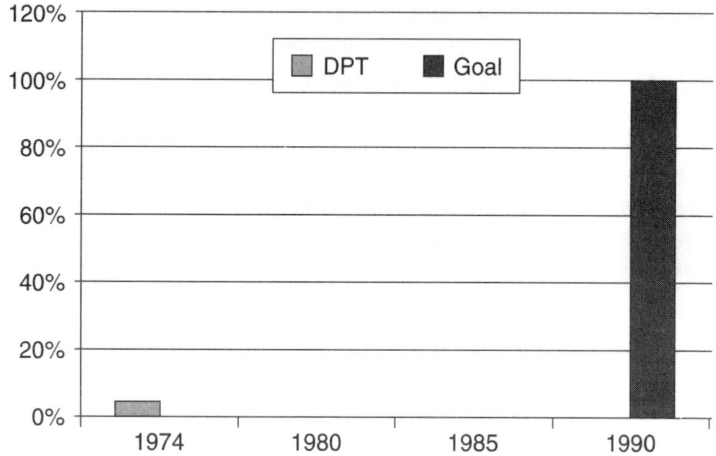

Note: I have not specified the DPT dose estimated for 1974: we really had little idea of coverage other than that it was extremely low.

It is customary for technical matters of this sort to be debated first in 'Committee A' of the Assembly before being passed to the full Assembly for endorsement. I was scheduled to introduce the report but I got lost in the labyrinth of the Palais des Nations, a sprawling complex dating from the time of the League of Nations, and was not there when the item came up. (They did not name the great hall the

'Salle des Pas Perdus'—hall of lost steps—for nothing!) Dr Mahler was not pleased! But I was able to give my 'introduction' at the end of the debate and answer the questions that had arisen at the same time. So, despite my faux pas, the EPI and I escaped without harm.

We also made it a priority to get the EPI Manual[3] cleared for release. It had been stalled for months because the section on motorcycle maintenance had been deemed inappropriate for WHO. Ko and John Lloyd had been adamant in wanting it included! They were field-experienced and field-oriented and wanted to meet the needs of the field staff. But I was forced to recognise that the tradition-bound bureaucracy of WHO was unlikely to yield. And we desperately needed that manual to provide the basis for our training course for national managers. So we sacrificed the section. The manual was issued and consultants from CDC's Bureau of Training turned it into a course for national managers that was conducted that fall in Kuala Lumpur, Malaysia.

The EPI had quickly spent the $160,000 initially donated by the Danish International Development Agency (DANIDA). But these funds kept miraculously reappearing! DA explained to me that this was due to the goodwill of Adriano Imbruglia, chief of BUD (the HQ budget unit), who replenished these funds from other unspecified contributions. He had taken similar action to help the smallpox programme—an example of the importance of making friends in key places! This support was critical to our survival, allowing us to build our technical base until we could compete for additional help from other donors.

Staffing Up

'Get the best people you can find, give them the resources they need and let them get on with the job.' This advice was given to me by DA in 1965.

I had the luxury of filling 12 staff positions—eight professional and four secretarial. I wanted both Ko and Cobi to stay. Ko began his public health career serving the Dutch government in postings in the western part of Papua New Guinea (then under Dutch control) and other areas in Indonesia. He then joined the smallpox programme and became the smallpox regional advisor in SEARO, WHO's South East Asian Regional Office. I had met Ko briefly in Lagos, Nigeria, in 1968 at an international smallpox meeting. DA had introduced us, giving him high praise.

We got along splendidly from the start, despite my being a decade younger (40 to his 50 years) and far less experienced. I was there because of CDC and US backing. Ko was already a staff member and had no institution championing him. He accepted the political reality. He also quickly learned how much I respected him and his advice. He was my mentor and my friend and his contributions to all aspects of the EPI were a major reason for its success. (He could also, if called upon, drink more beer than anyone I have ever known. He told a colleague that the first was for thirst, the second for taste and the third for pleasure—and we are talking litres here, people!)

Cobi was also Dutch and she and Ko were close friends. She was the EPI's first and sole secretary, who worked tirelessly doing whatever she could to help the programme. She could not have been a better choice for that position. But I soon discovered she had liabilities that presented problems for a larger unit. One example was the filing system. We were busy and did not want to have to ask Cobi for every document. She was not happy about our finding them without her. Perhaps an understandable reaction, but also symptomatic of a larger issue: she needed to be in charge and to protect her domain.

I explained my dilemma to Ko. We were establishing the senior secretarial post for the new unit. I felt Cobi would not do. We both knew that she was too proud to accept any lesser post. And we also knew she had deep loyalty to the EPI and would be deeply hurt if not selected. Ko's dilemma was undoubtedly far more painful than mine. Yet he did not protest at my decision to recruit someone else.

We chose Libby Girardet to be our senior secretary. From South Africa and with a university degree, Libby did a superb job of recruiting the other secretaries and in organising the unit to be efficient and user-friendly. She and her husband also organised our first EPI Runs (5 km run/walk events for colleagues), described later. As we had feared, Cobi took the decision extremely badly and left. She rejoined us several years later when she was selected for the post of administrative assistant, which gave her a measure of authority and independence. It was semi-sweet, as both she and the EPI had evolved and she could not again play the central role she had enjoyed before.

In filling other professional positions, I looked first to the existing staff at headquarters, where a transfer would be quick and easy. I approached Fakhry Assaad, who had contributed a lot during his part-time assignment. The problem was that he felt he should be designated as the senior medical officer in recognition of his long service to the WHO. But I felt Ko was more deserving of the position. Fakhry was one of the nicest individuals and I know his insistence on seniority was not really to challenge Ko, it was because he would lose face and could not do otherwise. He stayed in the Communicable Disease Division, later becoming director. He never diminished his support for the EPI.

Ehsan Shafa, an Iranian national, who had done outstanding work there in smallpox eradication, did join us from the HQ smallpox unit and helped with field visits before his retirement a year or so later. Our major catch, however, was John (Jock) Copland (from the US), the smallpox unit's administrative officer. Jock had been able to forge excellent personal relationships throughout the HQ bureaucracy and it paid off handsomely in removing obstacles relating to budget, personnel and office space. Jock continued this role for the EPI and he, Ko and I formed the unit's directing triumvirate.

Jock's history is irresistible. He graduated from Yale with a major in dance before joining the Marines (the Marines!) in the Korean War era. He tells with glee that one of his assignments was to perform 'short arm' inspections (e.g. inspections of the penis looking for signs of venereal disease) on his colleagues during a stint at a health/hygiene post. By our era, he was perfectly open about being gay and he and Norman Braden, his long-time partner, were warmly welcomed. Jock jokes about that era, but being gay and in the Marines in war must not have been all fun.

Carol Torel also deserves special mention. Born in Singapore, she had been in a business position before coming to us in about 1978. We needed a person to work full time on our information system (described later). There was undoubtedly an initial period of mutual disappointment. Carol came stylishly dressed and really had no innate feel for numbers. She appeared neither interested nor a hard worker. But Ko and Jock gave her patient coaching on what data were needed in what format and at what frequency. Within a month, she was working flat out, determined to succeed. The job required constant badgering of national managers to submit data and then badgering some more when there were obvious errors or discrepancies. She never did get a good sense of numbers, but more than made up for this by her scrupulous attention to detail. She was the right person in the right place at the right time!

Over the next several months we used consultants for short-term help while we built up the remainder of our full-time staff. The latter developed into a rich mix of nationalities, including American, British, Finnish, Latvian (technically Soviet), Polish and Russian (also technically Soviet). They were not atypical for HQ, including the absence of someone from a developing country.

One key to the success of the smallpox programme had been DA's ability to get the support of the Soviet Union, one price being the agreement to recruit Soviet staff. Thus the recruitment of our Russian (Val) and Latvian (Mike) personnel; they represented the extremes in terms of competence.

We soon learned from his continuous filing errors that Val, recruited as an 'administrator', could not read the English alphabet and that his main task was to keep close watch on us on behalf of the former USSR. He had had intensive language training in 'English' (we all assumed at the hands of the KGB) and spoke with a harsh accent over the phone that made people think he was an obnoxious American. We replaced him as soon as we could, of course taking care to maintain good relations with the USSR!

Mike was a medical officer, fluent in English and French. He was very competent and well-liked. He elicited unheard-of praise for HQ from Dr Comlan Quenum, the irascible director of the WHO Regional Office for Africa, for his work at the office in assisting them.

John Lloyd continued to receive support as a full-time consultant from the Overseas Development Agency (ODA). John's long-time friend and fellow architect, James Cheyne, had begun doing cold chain consultancies for us and UNICEF in late 1976, and in 1979 joined us full time, again thanks to ODA. However, it did not last long! Funding ended along with Margaret Thatcher's austerity budget. We knew we could not afford to lose these two and, very fortunately for us, DANIDA responded to our appeals and support continued. How many other institutions would support staff from another country!

Except in Europe, the regional EPI advisors were the former advisors for the smallpox programme. Some were better than others, but they all carried with them the smallpox spirit and certainly did what they could to help the EPI.

The Americas had no smallpox and so had not had an advisor. They appointed Ciro de Quadros (from Brazil) for the EPI. He had performed with high distinction in the smallpox programme in Ethiopia and did a superb job in rapidly improving the immunisation services in Latin America.

Our colleagues in the European Regional Office saw no need to do much about immunisation services there and made little effort to support the EPI, despite the shockingly little use of the measles vaccine and wide variation in the quality of national immunisation programmes, a situation that we were only able to partially remedy in later years.

Many other professionals came to help us as consultants to supplement our full-time staff. They were a marvellous resource. We could afford them only because we received good marks from the donor community which provided us with voluntary contributions. We were able to pay only partial salaries to those taking sabbaticals from universities in the US, or just per diem and travel for those associated with government institutions such as the CDC. John and James were especially creative in building a network of individuals skilled in addressing problems of cold chain and logistics. This was formalised into 'TechNet', still alive today.

We became a close-knit family. Ko was especially good at poking his nose in offices to look in on staff and offer help where he could. He did not like closed doors, and ours were generally open, something I was used to at CDC but that was not the norm in WHO. It was but one example of our exceptional *esprit des corps* and a demonstration of what could be done even in an environment in which so many were engaged in routine activities with little sense of urgency or excitement.

We engaged in a bit of staff deception, however. Frank Schofield, the ousted EPI coordinator, felt unfairly treated and sued for remediation. I think his complaint was basically that he had been doing an adequate job and had been replaced only because of political pressure from the US. His suit took some months, and was ultimately successful. We were concerned that Frank would be returned to us as the director of the EPI. Ko suggested to Jock and I that we take preventive action to help the unit as a whole deal with the consequences of Frank's return.

We asked Bill Barton, in charge of management training at HQ, to arrange a course in which we would all participate. We actually took a rather dim view of the benefits of this training so far as management was concerned, but thought group participation would help our morale. Bill, a former chief medical officer for the British colonial medical services in Kenya, was absolutely delighted that we wanted his services. The course was a smashing success in improving morale. Even better, it proved unnecessary as Frank never materialised, choosing other recompense. Neither Barton nor the rest of our staff ever learned our true motivation!

Supervisors

As division director, my direct supervisor was an assistant director-general (ADG, or AD'sG in the plural). The AD'sG are appointed by the director-general (DG), forming a bureaucratic layer between him or her and the division directors. Originally, by informal agreement, the five permanent members of the UN Security Council (China, France, Russia, the UK, and the US) were represented and that was the case when I joined WHO in 1977. (It has been less strict since.) They have usually numbered six to seven in total. Except for the ADG in charge of administration, they have (or at least had) little practical responsibility. But they can all say 'no', causing problems for the divisions under them.

One of the reasons DA cited to me in making his decision to leave WHO was the difficulties he faced in dealing with Dr Lucien Bernard, a French ADG, who was not a fan of the eradication effort. But in 1976, just as DA had decided to leave, Dr Ivan Ladnyi, a Ukrainian (Soviet) who had distinguished himself working for the smallpox programme in East Africa, replaced Bernard.

Ladnyi could not have been more supportive. He took some risks to keep us out of trouble. He took me aside one day to warn me about the activities of Val, our Russian staff member, who had dutifully reported to him about my 'disloyalty'. I had told the staff that I was concerned about flying on Aeroflot to a meeting in Ulaanbaatar, the capital of Mongolia. Ladnyi advised I be more discreet! He was also helpful in letting us say 'goodby' to Val.

Ladnyi was obliged to return to the USSR in 1981 and was replaced by friend and colleague Serguei Litvinov, who had formerly served as medical officer conducting the studies of the EPI and cold chain in Ghana (mentioned in Chapter 2). Serguei, like Ladnyi, was well-respected and gave us warm support. When he, too, was called back, his successor was a Russian (Soviet), previously working in the Communicable Disease Division. He was not highly regarded, but not obstructive. He wanted to travel to one of our meetings but, since the ADG offices do not generally have travel funds, he had to ask me for them. I refused, as he had nothing to contribute to the meeting and I had better uses for those funds. The EPI had come a long way!

As DG, Dr Mahler always gave the EPI and me strong support, although we had at least one uncomfortable encounter early on. In the fall of 1977, my sister and my father (editor of *Reader's Digest Condensed Book Club* at the time) made a visit to Geneva on their way to the Frankfurt Book Fair. Ilze and I took them to dinner at the Café de Paris, an informal and highly popular spot downtown. Pop asked if the job of the WHO director was political and I replied (in a loud voice, as he was across the table and it was noisy): 'It certainly is: the director-general is right now out politicking to persuade the executive board to re-nominate him in January.'

Well, the DG was not out of town. At that very moment he was directly behind me as he and his family were just seating themselves at the table next to us. I had not intended the remark to be pejorative, but there was no point in trying to explain. And I think it really hurt Dr Mahler, who was really the embodiment of selfless devotion to the WHO and primary health care, but who nevertheless had to do a modicum of showing that he was ready and willing to continue serving another term as DG.

Three years later, another meeting with Dr Mahler worked better. In late December 1980, when most staff at headquarters was on vacation, I was not. I learned that, because of the need for more office space, the EPI offices were to be moved across the street to the International Labour Office (ILO) building. I found Ladnyi and we went to Dr Mahler to protest. He explained that he had chosen us for the move because he knew of our high morale and thought we could take the move in our stride.

I said that we were perfectly willing to be moved but felt we should have been consulted first. Dr Mahler apologised, but said that many other directors would likely have created political problems by complaining to their embassies. I knew he felt badly that he had not warned us but I was also not above exploiting his feelings to ask for really good office space and, as even more reward, to be given the new WANG computers that were just then being introduced into the organisation. Ko actually welcomed the change as he believed, correctly as it turned out, that it would improve our team spirit even further, besides giving us prime office space and equipment.

About a year later, Dr Mahler joined us for a staff meeting. We were his first guinea pigs in an effort he was making to know the WHO programmes better. He put on quite a show! He chose to be provocative and made a point of scoffing John Lloyd's invention of the ice-lined refrigerator that was just then going into commercial production by Electrolux. (John had converted a top-loading chest freezer into a refrigerator by lining the walls with water-filled tubes. The thermostats were adjusted to permit the tubes to freeze and then to cut the power until refreezing was required. Melting of the frozen tubes maintained safe storage temperatures and these units could run on only eight hours of electricity per day.) Mahler recalled his own efforts to improve TB X-ray equipment that had all failed, in part because of the lack of a commercial market. (We did not take Mahler's challenge too seriously as UNICEF was already buying the refrigerators and they proved a big success.)

And then, just to provoke me, Dr Mahler described my unprofessional behaviour in the Café de Paris. I could only sit there and agree. Yet the move to ILO and the airing of the Café de Paris fiasco only strengthened our mutual appreciation that grew stronger with time. (Dr Mahler could later admit to Ilze and me of his embarrassment in being hit with 'Delhi belly' while addressing the staff in SEARO. He was soaked below the waist before his remarks were finished. Staff scrambled to get him washed and a new suit made. Although we have all had our moments, that performance was fully worthy of a director-general!

Significant Others

When I first came to Geneva, speculation was rampant about the fate of WHO's Biologicals Unit (BLG) that, among other functions, certified that medications and vaccines met WHO standards. It was rumoured that DA, before deciding to leave WHO, had planned to put the unit under his supervision along with the EPI. He had had a bruising battle with the US Bureau of Biologics in the late 1960s over the new standards they proposed that would have made the smallpox vaccine sterile. The problem was that virtually all of the vaccine produced in the world at that time entailed growing the virus on the skin of cattle (mainly calves) and achieving complete sterility was not feasible. DA was able to persuade the Bureau to drop this requirement, but I think the experience made him want to have the WHO unit under his control.

Dr Frank Perkins (a Yorkshire man) was chief of the BLG, and not a person to be trifled with. He did not take kindly to the rumour! As a new, young director, I really had no wish to take on Frank. He was competent and highly respected internationally and I had other problems to confront.

In addition, I thought that it was appropriate that we have the folks who used the vaccines (us) administratively separate from those who certified they were fit to use (Frank). This is consonant with the WHO principle that national authorities who certify vaccines and other products be independent of those who produce them. We stayed separate units and had excellent working relationships. After Frank and I had left the scene, however, the EPI and BLG were brought together within a single division, although remaining as separate units. To my knowledge, this has posed no problems.

I will mention the Global Advisory Group (GAG) later on. But many of the individuals and institutional representatives who participated in the GAG meetings also provided substantial technical and financial support to our efforts. These included representatives from the development agencies of Britain, Denmark, the Netherlands, Norway, Sweden and the US, as well as those from other institutions within these countries.

The CDC was one such institution that helped us with staff and resources, another was the International Children's Center (Paris). They helped us to conduct our first EPI management courses in French and helped us support national programmes in several Francophone countries in Africa. Rotary International, a non-governmental organisation (NGO), provided financial help and outstanding political leadership at the country level in supporting the EPI as a whole, while also providing support and advocacy for polio eradication, their principal focus. (Rotary support remains strong even today.)

These examples illustrate the more general point that WHO as a whole cannot function without substantial technical and financial support from national institutions and individual experts who are willing to help. The CDC example is extreme: it has become increasingly engaged in WHO programmes, starting with the secondment of a single staff member (D. A. Henderson) to WHO in 1966 and soon supplying staff to smallpox field positions. It seconded me to the EPI in 1977 and Dr Michael Merson to the Diarrhoeal Diseases Control Program in 1978, and has since sent staff to the field, to Regional Offices and to HQ to support a wide variety of initiatives. In some instances (such as with smallpox and polio eradication), the CDC involvement is so strong that it is in effect the implementing agency, although flying under the WHO flag.

Notes

1. Countries pay contributions to WHO's regular budget based on their resources, the least developed actually getting a net contribution. US wealth makes it the largest contributor, the 25 per cent representing a cap to prevent even larger dominance.

2. We really did not want to set any goal of less than 100 per cent; even if we only achieved a lower number, we should try to reach them all. Grant would later modify this to 80 per cent to give national leaders the sense that this could actually be achieved.

3. 'Immunize and Protect Your Child: EPI Manual', 1977.

4

THE COLD CHAIN

He who would do good to another must do it in minute particulars;
general good is the plea of the scoundrel, hypocrite and flatterer.

William Blake, Jerusalem, f55, II.48–53, 60–61

The World Health Organization (WHO) and UNICEF ushered in the era of Primary Health Care, the bold vision of essential health services for all, with their joint sponsorship of the 1978 conference in Alma Ata. This was general good, even if plead with the best of intentions. And, indeed, many individual demonstration projects succeeded, at least in the short term. But progress in general was terribly slow, and not helped by the fact that some countries appointed special primary health directors who tried to run what were in effect vertical programmes.

John Lloyd and James Cheyne (introduced in Chapter 3) dealt with the 'minute particulars'. John began our operations. He was travelling in East Africa in 1975 when he learned of an immunisation disaster unfolding in Tanzania: a measles epidemic was occurring among vaccinated children. The WHO representative, concerned by these cases, had tested this vaccine. He started at the periphery and traced back through the regional to the central stores. As he could find no potent vaccine at any site, he concluded it had been impotent on arrival. The vaccine had been donated by China, allergic in that era to having anything questioned or examined. The upshot was the dismissal of the representative! (No good deed goes unpunished!) John thought he could help prevent such tragedies and joined the

Expanded Program on Immunization (EPI) the next year to work on cold chain and logistics problems, beginning with the design of the cold box mentioned previously. He also started working with Electrolux to produce refrigerators more suited for tropical climates.

As he looked, he found problems everywhere! Most central stores in developing countries, even if they had adequate refrigeration, were not closely monitored. Shipments to regional stores, and finally to the health centres, had little protection. Anecdotes from India reported vials of DPT and BCG being stored in bananas (easily transported and, indeed, providing at least some insulation) or in the ground. At the health centre, the kerosene refrigerators that were the main standbys in rural areas were often out of service either because of lack of fuel or because of some maintenance or repair problem.

John found that in Indonesia, it was taking 18 months for a vial of DPT vaccine to reach a health centre from the central stores. And Egypt was producing 50 dose vials of tetanus toxoid. After a few injections, the rubber tops were perforated with holes, and bits of rubber could be seen in the vaccine itself. Sterilisation of needles and syringes was inadequate to non-existent.

The EPI Manual

John and Ko quickly realised that a thorough review of procedures and policies was needed. They set about writing a comprehensive manual to set standards that, in turn, allowed training courses to be developed and that also allowed both programme managers and suppliers of vaccines and equipment to plan. How many doses of each vaccine were needed? In what sized vials, taking how much storage space at what temperatures?

Answering these many questions required making decisions. While 'best practices' in industrialised countries could serve in some circumstances, they were not always consistent and not always the most suitable for developing countries. Maybe the length and gauge of the needles needed for intradermal, subcutaneous, or intramuscular injections did not all have to be individually specified, but standardising these was important for manufacturing and procurement. So a number of decisions were just choices between good options.

In some cases, however, the choice was more difficult, as in the case of the age for starting immunisation. The United Kingdom

(UK) and its Commonwealth countries began at three months of age while the United States (US) began at six weeks. The earlier start was more appropriate for developing countries, but Ko decided we should recommend three months as this was in more common use and would likely gain wider acceptance. On the other hand, he was willing for us to recommend a minimal interval between DPT and OPV of four weeks rather than the usual six to twelve weeks.

Ko presented his recommended schedule at a number of regional meetings at which other options were also discussed. No single schedule was supported by everyone and in the end Ko put his in the manual. But that schedule did not last long. We soon gained the confidence and the credibility to recommend starting immunisation at six weeks, not three months. Delaying or withholding immunisation in the developing world has lethal consequences.

The manual was a tour de force specifying detail after detail. It was our bible of standard operating procedures. As mentioned, it was the basis for the training courses that soon began. John did run into one unexpected problem, though. He could not find an illustration of an intradermal injection, a delicate procedure requiring a small needle that could place the vaccine just under the top layer of skin. Worse, none of the doctors he consulted could themselves demonstrate the procedure. Ever resourceful, he found a nurse at the United Nations Joint Medical Services who immunised the child of a staff member with BCG while he took notes and drew. The illustration from the manual is reproduced below (Figure 4.1).

Keeping Cool

John and James revolutionised the cold chains in the developing world within a few short years. John helped develop many new or improved products. James focused more on improving systems; they made a wonderful complementary team. UNICEF was a major partner in this development, in addition to its more general role in promoting and funding the EPI. John and James arranged for the testing of cold chain equipment by a consumer product testing laboratory in the UK and developed performance standards for each item. UNICEF then purchased the equipment meeting those standards. How novel to actually test items before purchase! Market incentives led manufacturers to meet or exceed the existing standards

FIGURE 4.1: Copy of Page from the EPI Manual

II.2
page 27

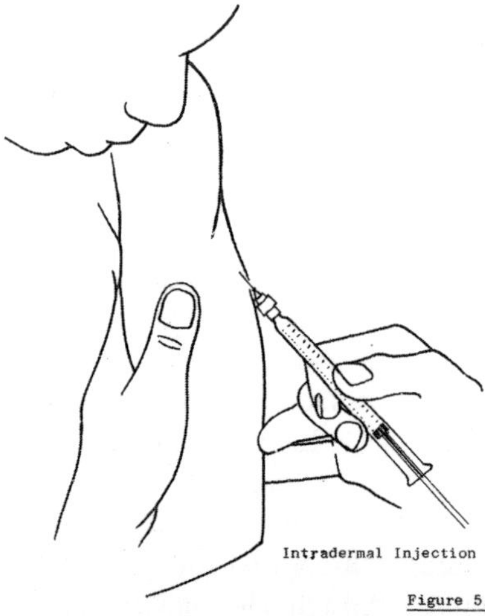

Intradermal Injection

Figure 5.3.8

If the skin is clean it need not be disinfected. If it is dirty, wipe it clean with a cottonwool swab moistened with water or methylated spirit; let it dry, then:

(1) Hold the upper arm firmly in the middle with your left hand, your fingers at the side of the child's body, your thumb at your side;

(2) With the fingers of your right hand, hold the syringe by the barrel (do not touch the plunger) with the ml. scale upwards and the needle in the direction of the child's shoulder.

that could then be raised to higher levels. They also prepared 'Product Information Sheets' that we distributed to national managers and non-governmental organisations (NGOs). They listed the manufacturers, the price and the performance of each item and helped improve the purchasing from sources outside of UNICEF.

Another breakthrough related to monitoring. Soon after joining the EPI in 1976, John learned that the 3M Company had developed a time/temperature monitor for use in the US domestic frozen food industry. The monitors had been developed in response to legislation pending during the Nixon administration that would have required them to be used in some food chains. But the legislation died with Nixon's resignation, and the food industry, with Union opposition, did not voluntarily accept the monitors. 3M was about to abandon them. Recognising their potential, John convinced 3M to adapt and manufacture the monitors for us.

The first ones consisted of a white strip of wax and an indicator dye (Figure 4.2). Pulling out a tag put the dye in contact with the wax, progressively colouring it. A white strip meant no break in the chain; a completely coloured strip meant a big problem! So long as the strips had not changed colour, they served for the entire length of the cold chain—from the manufacturer to the point of vaccine use.

FIGURE 4.2: One of the Cards John Designed

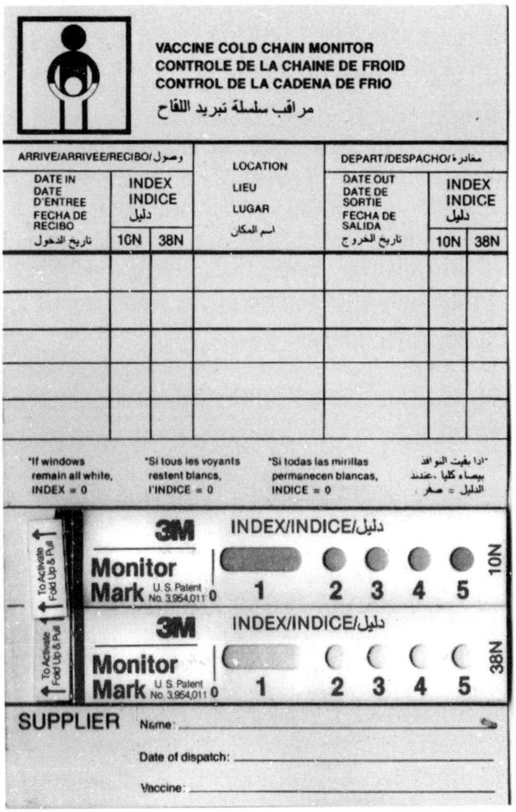

Note: This specific card is about 35 years old, but the photo is from June 2014. The strips turn completely blue after 48-hours exposure to temperatures above 10 and 38 degrees centigrade. Note that the tab on the top card is dislodged, although not completely pulled. That seems to have been sufficient for the card to turn blue, as designed. This card was soon replaced by a card with a single strip combining both functions, which is still being produced by Berlinger & Co.

UNICEF, following the pattern described above, soon required manufacturers to include monitors with their vaccine shipments. Over time, monitors have become more sophisticated so that an indicator dot can be placed on each vial of vaccine.

A number of studies of cold chain performance were carried out in Europe and the US using such monitors. Anthony Battersby, one of the TechNet mafia, was a leading investigator. He wrote to me recently with the following account (slightly edited) of some of these.[1] The studies were conducted between 1987 and 1991 (remember that freezing can inactivate DPT vaccine; heat, even only 25 degrees centigrade, can inactivate oral polio):

> The first was in Hungary that thought it had a brilliant cold chain. It did not. Romania was especially interesting: [the] vaccine was sent by train taking two weeks to travel 80 miles. In Bulgaria, the doctors decided to collect the vaccine rather than rely on the normal distribution. It was winter and they put the vaccines in the boot: all the DPT froze. In Tajikistan, where the ambient was –30°C, the vaccine was kept in the unheated section of the health center and all froze. [The] OPV was kept in the heated section where the temperature was in excess of +25°C.
>
> My initial visit to Moscow found that it was taking a week to get the vaccine from the vaccine institute to the railway station. In Dublin I opened a refrigerator to find thousands and thousands of doses of smallpox vaccine; this was in the late 1980s. In the UK, when I first reviewed the cold chain, the vaccine was being sent by post. This was soon changed to delivery direct from supplier to end user. In the Cantacuzino Institute in Bucharest the DPT was stored in the corridors of the Institute for months at ambient temperature after it had been released. These are just a few of the countries I assessed.
>
> I wonder what all these countries' cold chains look like today.

Given the above finding for products as special as vaccines, one would think these monitors would also be of interest in domestic food markets. But have you seen any in your grocery store lately? Probably not!

Of course, staff had to be trained to use the monitors and this was no problem. Yet, who would have imagined that an internationally respected head of laboratory services in Egypt would not understand? He showed no reaction when one of our staff showed him that the monitors in his central stores had all turned colour completely! When he finally did understand the implications, he promptly threw our staff member out! This was the same laboratory that was producing the 50 dose vials of tetanus toxoid.

New products were certainly a boon, but what was to be done to repair those refrigerators that populated developing countries? Kerosene powered many and they were notoriously difficult to maintain. But there were electric models as well and any given country had kerosene and electric models from many different manufacturers. James assessed which refrigerator brands were in most common use and then helped develop a kit with spare parts that would repair some 80 per cent of the problems. Not rocket science, you would think, but it had not been done before!

The kit was provided during repair courses for national staff. The first course, a photocopied draft produced in some three weeks, was given in Kathmandu, Nepal. It was revised over another 10 days and given again, and this cycle of use-revision-use was repeated a few more times until everyone was satisfied. We attempted such a quick turnaround in all we did. This was not the usual WHO approach, and one that is apparently even less typical today when so many initiatives are subjected to meticulous oversight and review. This is certainly a dilemma, as WHO cannot lose credibility. On the other hand, it has no credibility if it cannot act.

Not every idea generated in the unit triumphed, however. In Egypt (I am really not trying to pick on them!), John recommended that insulated container-trucks be used for transporting vaccines from Cairo to the regional stores. The trucks were put into service, but when John went to look at them he discovered that the workers had not realised that the trucks were not refrigerated. They required ice and the activation of their circulating fans in order to work. The workers thought that once they closed the doors, cooling would take place automatically, their faith unshaken despite the heat they found when the doors were opened. One could laugh (or cry) at this error, but we only had ourselves to blame: we had not provided any training.

Keeping Safe

Not only were many vaccines impotent at the time of administration, injection practices were unsafe. Large glass syringes were the norm in the 1970s, each piston being manufactured to fit a single barrel. They broke easily and it was common for a health centre to have only one or two, leading them to use the same syringe for multiple injections, changing or 'flaming' the needle between injections. The primitive sterilisation equipment available was generally a pan of water heated by an alcohol flame that did not provide sterilising temperatures. Moreover, the syringes and needles in the pan were scrambled so that it was a matter of chance whether or not the one withdrawn for next use was the one that had been most recently dropped in.

We were painfully aware of these problems. They remain a challenge in many settings, but we did make progress. In 1980, John convinced UNICEF to stop supplying glass syringes and instead use plastic syringes that could be sterilised in boiling water. We were soon getting reports, however, that these syringes were melting. So John had UNICEF change the specifications to require use of a high grade polypropylene. He then designed a portable steriliser, converting a domestic pressure cooker with syringe racks for the purpose (Figure 4.3). However, the device did have some teething problems! While testing the first prototypes in Kenya, the lid seal blew out on

FIGURE 4.3: Pressure Cooker Steam Steriliser for Syringes and Needles

one, spewing steam and sending it spinning across the room like a flying saucer! Thankfully no one was hurt and the problem never recurred. Since then, these pressure cooker sterilisers have worked so well that the industry making similar portable sterilisers is still active today.

But a second, even more serious, problem also existed. The syringes we were providing for immunisation were being reused without adequate sterilisation elsewhere within the health services and, worse, were finding their way into the hands of traditional healers. By 1984, with UNICEF, we shifted policy from sterilising syringes and needles to destroying them after a single use. John designed a shipping box that also served as a disposal box. After being filled with used syringes, it was set on fire and within 20 minutes the plastics had burned and the needles sank to a heat-softened epoxy that absorbed and trapped them. It could be safely handled and discarded or incorporated into building materials. UNICEF still ships syringes in a similar safety box. And yet, in many settings syringes and needles were not destroyed: they were much too valuable. We had to do more.

Once is Enough! Single Use 'Auto-destruct' Syringes

In 1984, UNICEF loaned us Peter Evans to work on developing 'auto-destruct' syringes. They had to become inoperable after single use despite any countermeasures. Peter had actually discussed this back in 1980 with Dr Steven Joseph, UNICEF Special Advisor for Child Survival and Health Programs. It seemed a good idea and Peter came up with a design. But when he tried to patent it, he discovered that there were dozens of auto-destruct syringes under patent going back 20 years. None was commercially viable, however.[2]

While Peter was working with a number of inventors, Lucy Cheyne told James of a newspaper article about a Swiss who had won a prize some years earlier for an auto-destruct syringe at the Salle International des Inventions, Geneva. It had been awarded by none other than our director-general, Dr Mahler! James and Peter visited the inventor in 1985 to inspect the syringe and were impressed, although that specific design still did not fully meet our requirements.

Soon after the meeting they issued a request for proposals for such syringes and were soon engaged in testing and retesting models.[3] The Program for Appropriate Technology in Health (PATH) joined in the effort with a design they had acquired and persuaded Becton Dickenson to consider production.[4] By 1987, UNICEF was able to issue contracts for auto-destruct syringes to Baxa and Becton Dickenson (Figure 4.4). They provided them free to any country that wanted them, changing this policy in 1990 to requiring most countries to pay at a cost of under $0.12 each.

FIGURE 4.4: The Soloshot[5] Syringe

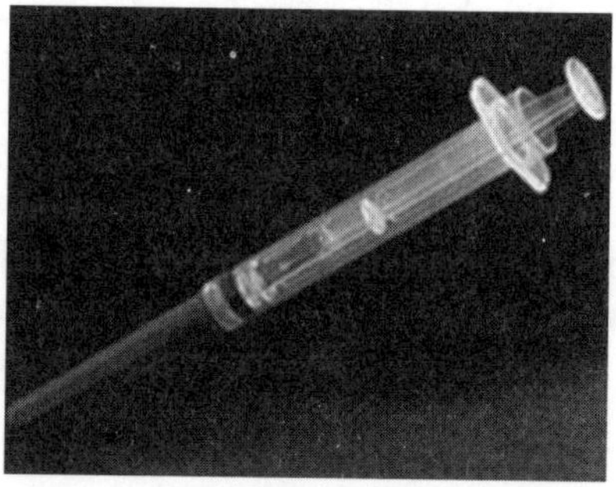

Note: The plunger can be withdrawn to fill the syringe. Once the direction is reversed, it cannot again be withdrawn.
Photo credit: PATH

Although WHO recommends the use of auto-destructs for all injections of essential medicines, little progress has been made to introduce them into curative services.[6] We await the next breakthrough. Perhaps it will be micro-needles? Each can contain a vaccine or other injectable. Multiple needles are applied to the skin on a small patch and the needles disintegrate, releasing their contents. A single patch can deliver a variety of vaccines and other products. A micro-needle flu shot is already in the market.

NOTES

1. Email correspondence, June 2014.
2. Email correspondence during 2012–14.
3. James Cheyne, in an email dated 10 September 2012.

4. PATH had its origins as an organisation promoting innovation in family planning in the 1970s and had expanded within a few years to supporting innovation in other areas of health. John Lloyd worked closely with them on a number of his projects and their support, as with this case relating to self-destruct syringes, helped get products from the design phase to commercial production.

5. Soloshot is a registered trademark of BD.

6. Email correspondence during 2012–14.

5

Management Nuts and Bolts

When the best teacher's work is done the people say 'We did it ourselves.'

Lao Tzu

If you don't know where you are going, any road will take you there.

A paraphrase from the dialogue between Alice and the cat in *Alice's Adventures in Wonderland*, by Lewis Carroll

Managing is basically the art of getting things done through others. Among its tools are training, monitoring and evaluation, and motivation. We had to develop each from scratch, adapting them as the programme grew. We were helped by the fact that we could measure immunisation coverage relatively easily and by the fact that failure to immunise was likely to result in epidemics of diseases such as measles or poliomyelitis. Measurement of failure is a great motivator, and perhaps the only sure way to achieve success!

Courses

That first course in Kuala Lumpur for national managers that we rushed into development in 1977 was designed to help them produce plans of operation. These were a prerequisite for obtaining donor support. The training approach was as important as the contents of the course. Most of it consisted of case studies with no clear solutions. After working on them, participants discussed their ideas together with a facilitator. Not only did participants learn, but they also felt empowered to do the tasks themselves. This course was soon followed by our second one, held for French speakers in Tipaza in Algeria.

We did not employ 'trainers' for these activities. We were our own trainers and 'we' included WHO HQ and regional staff, colleagues from other organisations, and national managers. We met together each evening to discuss progress and problems and to prepare for the next day. Our homework helped make us seem experts. But because the problems portrayed in the case studies had no single solution, our responses were not necessarily any better than those of the participants themselves. The mixing of international and national colleagues in these intense environments was powerful team-building. We were in this thing together.

All this turned out to be too much for a participant from South Korea in that first course. Few Koreans were permitted travel internationally then and those that were were highly stressed. They were expected to excel in all things, but a consequence was they often used alcohol and tranquillisers to excess. In our course there were few right or wrong answers, and he was expected to say what he thought. It was too much! He was found wandering in the hotel corridors one night, clearly having lost touch with reality. We had to refer him to our Malaysian hosts for care.

A side benefit from this training was that increasing numbers of participants became representatives attending the Executive Board and World Health Assemblies, where they were strong advocates of the Expanded Program on Immunization (EPI). This certainly did not hurt our standing within WHO and it also helped a great deal in letting donors know that their support was being put to good use.

As soon as our course for national managers was completed, we started work on one for the mid-level managers, again calling on our Centers for Disease Control and Prevention (CDC) colleagues, with the change that they were no longer at CDC. The Bureau of Training had been abolished! This course helped mid-level staff train and supervise front-line workers. And when that training was underway, the priority became 'micro-planning': courses for the front-line workers themselves focusing on the detailed logistics of supply and delivery.

James and Francois Gasse (another valued staff member who at various times worked both for WHO and UNICEF) also arranged to train UNICEF field staff. But WHO was not supposed to train

UNICEF staff, nor did UNICEF accept that they should be trained by WHO. So to save face on all sides, these events were simply called cold chain 'briefings'.

As the training efforts became more integrated within national programmes, UNICEF became an increasingly important source of funding. At the same time, UNICEF was increasing its provision of vaccines and other materials as the absorptive capacity of national programmes increased. Without the materials, the training would have been fruitless; without the training, much of the material would have been wasted. Training was a win-win investment for all.

I recall our colleagues at headquarters working with maternal and child health being extremely proud of publishing a book on best practices. They never translated it into training, but training was our lifeblood!

At the national level, indicators of the impact of the training included the dramatic improvement at all levels of the cold chain and improvements in providing safe injections, at least for immunisation. Another indicator was the increasing use of the EPI 30 cluster survey (discussed ahead) to assess immunisation coverage.

National Programme Reviews

We were strong proponents of conducting national programme reviews as they combined the functions of training, monitoring and evaluation and were highly rewarding for the participants. In addition, the international spotlight they provided helped to increase political commitment to immunisation within the countries that were the subjects of the reviews. Our approach was to have Ko or another senior staff member from an international or donor organisation lead the review, planning the details first with the national authorities and arranging for an independent mixed team of national and international staff (sometimes including national managers from another country) to actually perform the review. A coverage survey and a review of the cold chain and supervisory practices were always done and provided objective performance data. The effort was made to present the results in person to the Minister of the country in which the review had been performed.

At first, we tried to include our colleagues from headquarters who were responsible for primary health care in these reviews. We stopped trying, however, when they insisted that we include in our immunisation coverage survey questions (such as how far the nearest water source was to the household chosen in our sample) which they thought were interesting, but were actually irrelevant to the review. So we stopped doing anything with them. (Despite my efforts to get them to see the value of what we were doing in the area of cold chain and logistics, this seemed utterly irrelevant to them.)

The major drawbacks to our reviews were the resources they consumed. Aside from the time spent on planning, it took a week or more to complete the review and this was difficult for the senior staff involved. The main problem, however, was to find competent persons to lead the reviews. Ko was superb, but he could only lead so many. So we were only able to do a few before stopping completely. Fortunately, we could continue to get reasonably objective national data from the coverage surveys and cold chain monitoring, and we continuously fed this back to our WHO governing bodies and to the programmes themselves. This kept us grounded in reality. But as important as this was for motivation, it was no substitute for the reviews.

Monitoring and Evaluation

'You don't get what you expect. You get what you inspect.'

The 30 Cluster Survey

One of the most important assessment tools we used was a simplified survey method to estimate immunisation coverage. The original method had been developed at CDC by statisticians Robert Serfling and Ida Sherman (Serfling and Sherman 1965). It requires a meticulous selection of a sample population. Bill Foege, having just returned to CDC from Eastern Nigeria, and colleague Don Eddins had simplified it in order to conduct a coverage survey in Gambia in 1967. I made further shortcuts for my surveys in 1968.

The basic method goes step-wise, first randomly selecting 30 different areas or 'clusters' (for us, these were mainly villages). The selection is done so that larger areas have more chance of selection than smaller ones. After a cluster has been selected, randomly selected households are visited for interview. Done correctly, this ensures that each individual has the same probability of being chosen.

Reliable population data were scarce in West Africa, to say the least. Information was mostly limited to large towns or villages, but often based on a census conducted years in the past. And smaller areas did not make it to any central list. So we just had to do the best we could, estimating population sizes and including new areas we discovered on our visits.

After choosing our 30 clusters, we randomly selected a first household and then visited those nearby. The survey team would go to the centre, or what seemed to them the centre, of the cluster and choose a direction 'randomly', often by spinning a bottle. We counted the households in that direction and chose one randomly, one method being to choose the first number or numbers appearing on a currency note. After interviewing there, the team would move to the next nearest household (usually either to the right or the left) and continue doing so until the number of individuals required for that cluster had been interviewed.

It was certainly simple, but it was not really random, even if all the population figures had been accurate. For example, households towards the centre have a better chance of being selected than those near the periphery. The *Bulletin of the World Health Organization* published the method and the results from five of these simplified surveys conducted in the late 1960s in West Africa in 1973.[1]

One can forgive the statisticians for not being impressed! Nothing more was heard of this approach until I joined the EPI. I was happy to accept the method's flaws if its simplicity would get it used in immunisation programmes. It had served our purposes well in West Africa, where almost any estimates were way better than none. And for immunisation coverage, especially at first, we wanted a method that would be easily understood and widely applied, not necessarily a method of high accuracy.

So this became the 'EPI method' that we taught in our courses for senior and mid-level managers. They could use it themselves without having to call for help from census workers or statisticians. It became a standard element of national immunisation programmes and soon thereafter began to spread to other uses. During the decade of the 1980s, hundreds, if not thousands, of these simplified surveys were conducted.

The method worked far better than might have been expected. In 1982, we were able to analyse the results of 60 surveys conducted in 25 countries. We made computer simulations to test it on populations intentionally constructed to make it perform least well (Henderson and Sunderasan 1982). It had been designed to provide estimates of coverage that were within 10 per cent of the true value 95 per cent of the time. In both the actual surveys and the simulations, they did just that.[2] Since then, a number of papers have reviewed simulation and field studies pertaining to the method.[3] They show that more rigorous methods provide better results in terms of statistical validity and precision of the estimates. But the EPI method worked satisfactorily. It was a good tool for the purposes for which it was developed.

The 'gold standard' for such surveys is the Demographic and Health Survey (DHS)[4] developed by the United States Agency for International Development (USAID) from work during the 1960s to examine issues related to family planning. It is a superb tool, but so expensive it can only be performed after long intervals of several years. The Multiple Indicator Cluster Survey (MICS) developed by UNICEF in the wake of the 1990 World Summit for Children is less daunting and is currently being systematically done in 50 to 60 countries every five years.[5] But neither of these methods really meets the needs of the programme manager who wants a quick and inexpensive estimate of coverage.

The widespread use of cell phones offers a way of combining simplicity with rigor. They are being programmed so as to guide fieldworkers to houses that have been selected randomly. Data directly entered into the phone are collated centrally and automatically analysed. This allows quite complicated survey designs to be used without making the fieldwork itself difficult. This also permits the wider application of more rigorous survey methods. While our simple EPI approach may be supplanted, the spirit it embodies does live on! Managers of immunisation programmes consider estimates of coverage essential and will continue to gather data using methods that best meet their needs.

The Quarterly Objectives

Within our unit at headquarters, we used a system of quarterly objectives that I had been taught in an American Management

Association course. I took the course while at CDC and introduced the system within the Venereal Disease Control Division (henceforth VD Division). I took it with me to the EPI. Professional staff set objectives for themselves for each quarter and for the next three quarters. And each quarter we reviewed what we had actually accomplished the past quarter and looked at our priorities for the coming quarters. A truncated copy of an actual page from 1986 is given in Box 5.1.

> Box 5.1: Quarterly Planning/Performance Summary
> *Reporting date*: 10 January 1986
>
> 1. PREVIOUS QUARTER'S OBJECTIVES (October–December 1985)
>
> 1.1 General
>
> (1) Prepare training aid for mothers emphasizing child spacing and nutrition and TT immunization during pregnancy (Hamunen, et al.)
> *Target date*: 15 October 1985
> *Comments*: Delayed due to heavy work load of Janet Moore. Moved to current quarter.
>
> (2) Draft broad outline for 1990–1996 EPI MTP for discussion with Regional Advisors in Copenhagen (Keja, et al.)
> *Target date*: 25 October
> *Comments*: Accomplished.
>
> (3) Prepare agenda for session scheduled with Regional Advisors in Copenhagen (Keja, et al.)
> *Target date*: Provisional agenda by 25 October, final agenda to be developed with Regional Advisors during initial days of the GAG meeting.
> *Comments*: Accomplished.
>
> (4) Follow-up with UNICEF concerning EPI vaccine leaflets from manufacturers (Chan)
> *Target date*: 31 October
> *Comments*: Discussed with Peter Evans. UNICEF has incorporated EPI leaflet specifications into their vaccine tenders and anticipate conformity by manufacturers. Dr Clements will also review conformity....

Those objectives were the bane of my existence! They were supposed to reflect items beyond the routine; items that reflected initiative and challenge. I had a hard time formulating my own. Then I had to badger staff to submit theirs—they had no fewer problems than I! Then I reviewed, edited and consolidated them, often going back to the staff member involved to discuss revisions before we discussed them together in a staff meeting.

I really struggled with the whole process but once a quarterly cycle had been completed, I always felt that the gain had been worth the pain, if only just. Many times we failed to achieve what we had promised ourselves, but that was just fine. The point was to try. If the target date had to be postponed, OK. Or if the objective had to be dumped in the light of experience, OK again. The issue was to try to formulate and then discuss together what we would like to achieve without blaming anyone for failure. Self-criticism provided all the motivation needed. The exercise as a whole forced me to review each professional's work, including my own, and our open discussions together certainly helped us all understand what we were doing.

As our staff grew larger, the objectives consumed more and more time and I am not sure what would have happened had I remained much longer as director. When Bob Kim-Farley replaced me in 1990, he continued the objectives, but added some additional wrinkles, including heavier reliance on computer processing. But I think his personal investment was nowhere nearly as intense as mine and the objectives were soon abandoned. As assistant director-general, I encouraged the division directors reporting to me to try the system, but there were no takers. And I did not push. Their usefulness is very dependent on the user! James Cheyne has recently told me that he had found them highly motivating and had introduced them himself in a Gates-PATH project in 2000.

The EPI Information System

Our information system was, of course, a central element in our monitoring and evaluation activities. We needed the data from national programmes for our own analysis and we needed to report progress to Member States and to our many donors. I have mentioned Carol Torel's important role in this process previously (see Chapter 3).

I did, however, have one problem. WHO had designated one Salah Mandil to oversee the overall information system at headquarters. He was from a Middle Eastern country and was bright and affable with his male professional colleagues. But he was utterly disrespectful of women. Not only would he refuse to collaborate with women in professional grades, but it was also extremely difficult to find a secretary who could tolerate him. As if that were not enough, he kept over-promising what he could deliver. An example was a directory for headquarters that never seemed to materialise!

In any case, Salah decreed that we all had to conform to his information system at headquarters, even though it did not meet our needs. So I simply invented a new title for it—'The Special Purpose Information Sub-system (SPISS)'. It did not conform to the overall system, but Salah accepted that it was 'special' and allowed us to do what we wanted. Problem solved! So often one can find a way around a rule rather than opposing it directly. (Salah would soon be replaced by a lady, a big change for the better and universally welcomed.)

In addition to our reports to the Executive Board and World Health Assembly, we used WHO's Weekly Epidemiological Record (WER) to provide occasional updates on various activities. It is disseminated widely to national ministries of health and other interested parties. The smallpox programme had been an innovator in using WER and we simply followed their example. The WER also became our major means for publicising the recommendations of our Global Advisory Group (GAG). This gave the recommendations, as well as GAG itself, high credibility (more on this ahead).

We also created a special publication—*EPI Update*—to provide feedback from us to national managers (Figure 5.1). I did not want the typical chatty 'newsletter' with comments from the field, and this was, in part, to keep it short so it would be read. Also, I wanted it to be a management tool that allowed us to provide a clear focus on problems and progress. We provided a 'league table' in each issue showing some aspect of national results to spur competition. Individual issues were devoted to specific topics such as coverage, safe injections, poliomyelitis, and missed opportunities. It was not an easy document to produce, however. Although we tried for one issue per quarter, we often failed to meet our deadlines. The newsletter continued to be published until 1997.

Our information system failed in one major area, however: providing trends on the incidence of the diseases we were targeting. The Americas were the exception. The WHO Regional Office for the Americas was and is, of course, an exceptional regional office. It is also the Pan American Health Organization (PAHO). PAHO

FIGURE 5.1: Copy of the Front Sheet from One of the Newsletters

UPDATE

MAY 1988

Expanded Programme on Immunization

1948 40 1988 WHO/OMS

Monitor the Cold Chain – The Lifeline of the EPI

... monitoring the cold chain...

Highlights

- The cold chain ensures that potent vaccines are available at the right time, at the right place in the right amount.
- PEOPLE and EQUIPMENT make up the cold chain.
- Monitoring makes sure that the cold chain works.
- Monitor cards and freezewatch indicators are "silent supervisors":
  - — Monitor cards warn when vaccines have been exposed to temperatures too high.
  - — Freezewatch indicators warn when vaccines have been exposed to temperatures too low.
- A simple shake test can tell if DPT, DT or TT vaccines have been frozen.
- The quantity of vaccines available should be monitored using vaccine stock graphs. A reserve stock of 25% of the amount normally used between vaccine deliveries should be maintained.
- Monitoring the cold chain should assure that every dose administered is potent and that no woman or child is sent away because of lack of vaccine. It helps people to gain and maintain confidence in the health services.

WORLD HEALTH ORGANIZATION

Source: Reproduced with permission from the World Health Organization, Geneva.

was founded in 1902, well before WHO itself (1948). Before aligning itself with WHO, PAHO insisted on retaining its separate budget and on appointing its own regional director. It is because of this precedent that all regional directors in WHO are elected from within their regions and not appointed by the director-general. This is undoubtedly beneficial to PAHO, but not such a success elsewhere.

PAHO has more resources than do the other regions and its member states are relatively advanced. These factors facilitated the efforts of Dr de Quadros, who rapidly improved the reporting of cases of the EPI diseases. He was driven by the vision of eliminating poliomyelitis from the Americas, and the EPI was doing just that. The rapid decrease in cases helped him to convince the PAHO Directing Council to adopt that goal in 1985. Improvement in measles reporting soon followed, paving the way for the 1994 PAHO goal of regional measles elimination.

The European region mainly ignored the EPI. (This changed when George Oblapenko, a Russian friend who had previously worked in the Diarrhoeal Diseases Control Program or CDD in Geneva, led their successful polio elimination efforts in the early 1990s.) The other regions had far weaker national infrastructures and their disease reporting was dismal. I said at the time that if the trend lines we could show from our incoming data were lines on an encephalogram, the patient would be dead.

I tried to think of how, at the global level, we might get at least some crude indications of the impact of the immunisation services on disease incidence. In my Epidemic Intelligence Service (EIS) training I had learned that, for at least part of the surveillance of flu-like illness, CDC relied on weekly reporting from 122 cities chosen throughout the United States. They counted death certificates for which pneumonia or influenza was listed as the underlying or contributing cause.

Why not try something similar for measles and perhaps pertussis? We could try getting reports, perhaps on a monthly basis, from the principal hospital in the capital city of several large developing countries. So we tried what we called local area monitoring (LAM).

It failed miserably! For a start, it turned out to be extremely difficult to obtain hospital data. It requires much more time and effort than I had imagined. We actually had to send Ko to try to get data from Jakarta, Indonesia. Even he, with all his experience and persuasiveness, had difficulties. We had to drop the effort. Even so, undoubtedly because of Ko's efforts, the Ministry of Health in Indonesia did try to initiate such a system within the country, but that too was soon abandoned.

The fundamental issue, for our routine reporting and for our LAM, was that no one really cared. The reports were not generating action. The contrast to situations where the agreed goal is disease transmission elimination (local or regional) or eradication (global), is striking. Every case counts and reporting does make a difference.

The Global Advisory Group (GAG)

The Prince who is not himself wise cannot be wisely advised.
For good advice depends upon the shrewdness of the Prince
who seeks it and not the shrewdness of the Prince on good advice.

—Nicolo Machiavelli, *The Prince*

I had created an advisory group for the Venereal Disease Control Division way back when I was the division director at CDC in the early 1970s. The fact that I then disbanded it after it had become unproductive did not dissuade me from establishing one for the EPI when I arrived in 1977. We needed an outside group of experts to advise us and, in turn, to give added weight to any recommendations we might make.

The WHO has a well-recognised system of expert committees for just these purposes. But the rules of procedure are rigid and cumbersome. Before the members of an Expert Committee can be selected, an Expert Advisory Panel must be established from which the selection is made. There are formal rules of procedure for the meetings themselves and for the finalisation of the meeting reports. The reports are edited and formally published, a time-consuming process. In practice, such committees meet only every few years and their reports are published only months after they meet.

We needed something more flexible that would allow annual meetings and rapid dissemination of our recommendations. The Global Advisory Group or GAG we created was, I believe, the first of its kind within WHO (but by no means the last). It had 12 members, six chosen from the six WHO Regions (often national EPI managers) and the remaining six 'at large' (often credible immunisation experts). Each served a three-year term with the initial appointments staggered to allow for a turnover of a third of the members each year.

The selection of a competent and prestigious chairperson was essential. Enter Professor Jan Kostrzewski, Minister of Health and Social Welfare, Poland. A rower in the 1936 Berlin Olympics, he and a colleague had an adventurous and hazard-filled journey afterwards, trying to thread their way back home through the social chaos surrounding them. Later, during the Nazi occupation of Poland, he had worked in a vaccine production laboratory and had made sure that the vaccines destined for the occupiers lacked potency. He was a founder of the International Epidemiology Association in 1954 and was respected throughout Europe for leadership skills and wise advice. He had been a strong supporter of the Smallpox Eradication Programme and a vocal advocate for the EPI during the World Health Assembly debates in 1974 during which it had been established.

If we were delighted by him, he was not so impressed by me, nor was he impressed by the immunisation services in the US! So in June 1977, soon after I first met him, he set up a visit for me to Poland to see how an immunisation service really should be run. I was certainly impressed. Yet my time in West Africa, where I had seen first hand almost every catastrophe that can befall a programme, was even better preparation for the EPI. In any case, the trip dispelled any doubts he had about me and he accepted our offer to chair GAG.

The first GAG meeting was held in Geneva for three days in November 1978, with most of the 43 participants coming from headquarters (HQ) or the regional offices. All the subsequent meetings took five days and were rotated among the regions and HQ. By 1983, there were 76 participants with 26 (other than the GAG itself) coming from outside of WHO. These mostly represented the donor community and included Rotary International. The meetings were the major event of the year for us and I laboured from one meeting to the next to provide an agenda and background papers. It paid off.

We had the good fortune to have many prestigious individuals give their time to serve as GAG members. They took their roles seriously, and with good reason: their recommendations were taken as gospel and became 'best practices' for immunisation programmes in developing countries. Of course, there were differences of opinion, but they rarely reflected personal or political biases.

Reaching compromise was almost always possible, facilitated by the diplomatic and multilingual Kostrzewski. We took care in drafting recommendations as the meeting progressed (often amending drafts we had prepared beforehand) and had a final version ready for review and approval before the meeting's end. We made sure they were published within a few weeks in WHO's WER to reach both senior health ministry staff and national programme managers.

The GAG recommendations covered many issues, including the problem of 'drop outs', the need to reduce 'missed opportunities' for immunisation, and the importance of ensuring safe injections and maintaining the cold chain. GAG endorsement allowed developing countries to feel confident when adopting policies that differed from those in industrialised countries. One example was to give a polio dose at birth. It does not work as well as one given later, in part due to the interference from maternal antibodies. But it does have an impact, and contact with a child at birth or shortly thereafter in high risk environments is an opportunity not to be missed. Another was to immunise sick children! I better explain.

In 1983, a GAG report stated, in part, '...it is particularly important to immunize children with malnutrition. Low grade fever, mild respiratory infections or diarrhea, and other minor illnesses should not be considered contraindications...' (*Wkly Epidem. Rec.* 1984: 59, 85–89). Immunisation of children so sick as to require hospitalisation was not recommended. Studies in Kenya, however, had shown the risks children faced on entering wards filled with measles cases. So when there was danger of acquiring measles in the ward, we did recommend immunising sick children with the measles vaccine.

What a contrast with industrialised countries! The former Soviet Union provided an extreme example of the definition of a contraindication, refusing children immunisation on almost any pretext. Reusing or delaying immunisation without good reason can have dire consequences in any country, but is especially hazardous where the risk of disease is high.[6]

The review and discussions of the EPI during these meetings seemed to reassure our donors. They were active participants and acted not as 'outsiders' criticising, but as 'insiders' helping us to solve problems. One indication of this was that we were never asked to be the subject of a formal, donor-organised, external review such as had befallen the CDD that was so similar to us in other ways. That programme, however, had no counterpart to our GAG, and I think it was seen by donors as being less open about its activities, good and bad. We were grateful for this omission, as these reviews can be time consuming and aggravating. But we also had a low opinion of their effectiveness, mainly because of the difficulty in finding competent review leaders.

From time to time I attended advisory group meetings convened by the Maternal and Child Health Program. The contrast was striking. The meetings were not well-prepared, the chair was poorly briefed, and the results were not meaningful. The secretariat was not itself wise; it was not clear what it wanted.

We were a pretty motivated group at headquarters, as we saw success in moving the EPI forward. However, we also received an unexpected boost. Libby Girardet joined us in 1977 and she and her husband Guy suggested we start an 'EPI run'—a 3 km run, walk and picnic event.

Before coming to Geneva, they lived in a community in which these were used to promote spiritual growth. We began with a handful of participants from the EPI and CDD, reserving a nearby municipal picnic facility with a suitable trail. Even for our motley few in the first run, Libby and Guy measured the length of the course meticulously and had provided for timing the finishers, providing professional touches so essential for serious runners.

Each year our numbers and the number of WHO programmes represented increased. And we did, indeed, attract serious runners in addition to our walkers and family onlookers. We generally held the runs on weekdays in the latter part of September, before the time changed or the weather turned cold. Within a few years we had outgrown our original facility and had moved to a formal municipal sporting facility complete with track and restaurant. Now we also had others coming from the broader United Nations family. Cups and other awards were given to winners, with more and more categories by age and sex being added, as well as special children's events. It was a spectacular success and great morale builder for all concerned. It became the 'World Health Run'.

Within the EPI itself, most of the staff was engaged. For those first runs, John Lloyd designed T-shirts and we sold them slightly over cost to raise enough funds for rent and incidentals so that the event could be self-supporting. Other staff got sponsorship for food and trophies, prepared numbers for the runners, measured and otherwise checked the course, developed the software to analyse the results and attended to a hundred other details. The run was finally abandoned in 2001 when there were insufficient volunteers to carry the (considerable) burden—an unfortunate example of becoming too big *not* to fail.

Notes

1. See Henderson et al. 1973. The 'central' bias is caused by selecting households along a straight line. One should really select from a 'wedge' that contains more households at the periphery than in the centre.

2. In the actual surveys, in which true coverage was estimated to vary from a low of 5 per cent to a high of 94 per cent, 83 per cent had 95 per cent confidence limits within +/– 10 per cent. When true coverage was between 45 per cent and 54 per cent, only 50 per cent of the results were within the +/– 10 per cent confidence limits, but none of the surveys, no matter what the true coverage, had confidence limits exceeding +/– 13 per cent. In the simulated surveys, in which true coverage varied between 60 per cent and 87 per cent, 95 per cent were less than +/– 10 per cent from the true coverage and none exceeded 13 per cent.

3. See Bennett, et al. 1994; Lemeshow, et al. 1985; Lumen, et al. 2008; Milligan, et al. 2003. The actual SRS technique selected seven households as opposed to one in the EPI method. (Only seven children were needed in the sample.) If a child was not in the selected household then, as with the EPI method, the next household was visited until one child was found.

4. See www.measuredhs.com.

5. See www.unicef.org/statistics/index_24302.html.

6. Parents are in a pickle where successful immunisation has removed the disease threat! Do they refuse the vaccine, leading to more susceptible children and the risk of disease returning, or do they accept the vaccine, knowing it has rare adverse reactions? The quandary is made worse by the promulgation of unfounded alarms, such as that measles immunisation is associated with autism. The better our immunisation programmes, the more such challenges arise.

Part 3

Acceleration

6

Creating the Coalition

Salk's Gambit

For if the trumpet give an uncertain sound,
who shall prepare himself to the battle?

—1 Corinthians, 14.8

Did we ever have trumpets! They were Salk, McNamara, Mahler and, none more certain, Grant. We ourselves actually blew the first note, however. By 1980, we had prepared the ground and were now ready to move towards our 1990 goal of reaching all children. We could now begin to estimate global immunisation coverage as being about 20 per cent for a third dose of DPT; about 5 per cent in the least developed countries (LDCs) (Figure 6.1).[1] That signalled the need to get more resources into countries. Dr D. A. Henderson suggested we get James P. Grant, the newly appointed executive director of UNICEF, on board. We paid him a visit; Grant was sympathetic, but not enthusiastic. He was far more impressed by oral rehydration salts (ORS). He carried a packet in his pocket and extolled their virtues at every opportunity. He was captivated by the simple technology and the manifest 'doability' (one of his favourite words) of getting the salts to where they were needed. Immunisation was more complicated, but subsequent events would change his mind.

The next thing we tried was to use the World Health Assembly (WHA) to sound an alarm about our slow rate of progress. We prepared a report from the director-general warning that our 1990

FIGURE 6.1: Immunisation Coverage Estimates, 1974–80

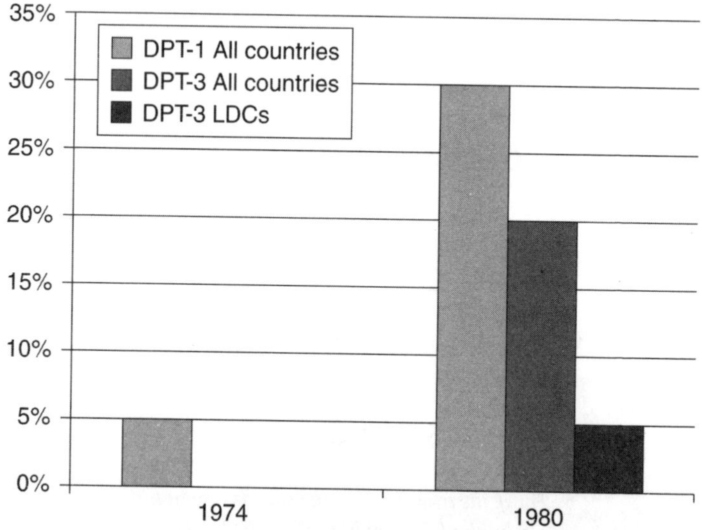

universal coverage goal was in jeopardy. The Assembly's resolution (WHA35.31) in May 1982 repeated that warning and endorsed a 'Five-Point Action Plan' to address the problem.[2] This provided an opportunity for Jonas Salk to enter and save the day!

Salk promoted the notion that using his inactivated polio vaccine (IPV) in a simplified two-dose delivery strategy would meet the 1990 goal. He had been working with the Institut Mérieux laboratories in Lyon, France (now BioMérieux) and the Netherlands Vaccine Institute at Bilthoven (now Bilthoven Biologicals) to adapt to polio virus the technique the latter was using to cultivate the whooping cough pathogen *Bordetella pertussis*. They were using large aerated tanks of liquid to grow the organisms.

For polio virus production, Styrofoam beads were added to the vats. The beads presented an enormous surface area on which these viruses could grow, producing the quantities needed for IPV far more cheaply than had previously been possible. Even with this new technology, the Salk vaccine remained more expensive to produce than the Sabin OPV. Only small quantities of virus are needed for a dose of OPV as it grows in the intestine to generate the immune response needed. But Salk proposed making savings to offset the IPV cost by having mobile teams visit communities only twice a year to provide two doses, rather than the minimum of three visits (and three doses) recommended by the EPI.

He set out to demonstrate this approach. He recruited Dr Hans Cohen, the director-general of the Netherlands National Institute of Public Health and Hygiene, who persuaded the Dutch Ministry of Development to help fund studies in Upper Volta (now Burkina Faso), Senegal and Mali. They were intended to show that this two-dose, mobile approach could eliminate polio. Charles Mérieux also supported these studies financially and ensured they were conducted under the auspices of the Association for the Promotion of Preventive Medicine, an organisation he created and funded. Philippe Stoeckel, a Mérieux operative, was its head. They hoped that if these projects succeeded, IPV and a two-dose delivery schedule would be widely adopted. This, of course, would be highly profitable for Mérieux laboratories and a delight for Salk in seeing his vaccine applied.[3]

I had the opportunity to join Salk and Stoeckel in a visit to a health post in Senegal to view one of these demonstration projects. It was a scene to delight any tourist! Our celebratory entrance to the village was marked by dozens of small children dutifully lining the dirt road and waving small flags. The festive occasion was only slightly spoiled when Philippe inadvertently slammed Salk's fingers into a car door. Salk was very impressed with all he saw, nonetheless.

By 1982, with preliminary results from these studies in hand, Salk approached Dr Ken Warren, director of the Health Sciences Division of the Rockefeller Foundation, to promote his idea. Ken approached Jim Grant and they, in turn, approached Robert McNamara, who had just retired from being president of the World Bank. So far, so good! McNamara was convinced that the donor community would contribute $100 million to support immunisation in developing countries. It was not a carefully selected amount, but a good round figure that seemed reasonable. And from McNamara's perspective, with his experience at the World Bank, a pittance. But McNamara insisted that the World Health Organization (WHO) also be involved. That was not good news for Salk! It was decided to hold a meeting of donors at the Rockefeller facilities in Bellagio, Italy, jointly sponsored by the Rockefeller Foundation, the World Bank, WHO, the UNICEF and the United Nations Development Fund (UNDP). The meeting was ultimately held in March 1984.

I was party to one of the planning meetings for this conference, accompanying Mahler. An item came up that pertained directly to the EPI and I offered my opinion relating to some technical point. The opinion might or might not have been relevant, but it became clear that I was not there to express one. McNamara squashed it as though it was an insect. No rancour, just utter dismissal. He was a powerful presence! (After Bellagio, when the EPI was really thriving, Bill Foege and I were sitting together in a meeting McNamara was addressing and he was kind enough to salute us both, as people who could get something done. I felt better about his previous rejection.)

Clash of the Titans

Prior to the convening of that first Bellagio Conference, Mahler and Grant found themselves in conflict. In 1978, using as a model the success of China's 'barefoot doctor' programme that Mao Zedong initiated in 1968, WHO and UNICEF jointly sponsored the International Conference on Primary Health Care (PHC) in Alma-Ata (now known as Almaty), USSR. The Alma-Ata Declaration specified the 'eight essential elements' of PHC: health education; promotion of adequate food supply and proper nutrition; adequate supply of safe water and basic sanitation; maternal and child health care, including family planning; immunisation against the major infectious diseases; prevention and control of locally endemic diseases and appropriate treatment of common diseases and injuries; and provision of essential drugs.

But it soon became apparent that this was a lot easier said than done. In 1979, Julia Walsh of Harvard and Ken Warren of the Rockefeller Foundation wrote a paper published in the *New England Journal of Medicine* proposing what they called 'selective primary health care' (Walsh and Warren 1979). Jim Grant, super salesman that he was, quickly transformed this into the quick-fix slogan of GOBI: Growth monitoring, Oral rehydration, Breast feeding and Immunisation, and featured this approach in the 1982–83 *The State of the World's Children* report (UNICEF 1982). Within a short time, this was expanded, adding 'FFF': Family planning, Female education, and Food supplementation (iron, folic acid and vitamin A).

Mahler was not happy, despite supporting the EPI and, later, the diarrhoeal diseases control programme as separate programmes within WHO. In an address to the WHA in 1983, he referred to such selected initiatives as 'red herrings'. He perceived them as a threat to his vision of a comprehensive health and development programme within a broad agenda for social justice. This very public and well-publicised statement did little to help collaboration between the two organisations, not always the best in any case.

In the fall of 1983, Mahler and Grant approached Bill Foege.[4] They were concerned that their individual egos were getting in the way of promoting the kind of cooperation that they both desired. They thought that Bill, heading some sort of independent group, might help absorb differences and promote collaboration. This occurred in the midst of the preparations for the Bellagio Conference.

On Lake Como: The First 'Bellagio' Conference: Protecting the World's Children, March 1984

Mountains will roar: what's born? A ridiculous mouse!

—Horace, 'The Art of Poetry'

There were only 34 participants, a choice dictated by McNamara and facilitated by the limited accommodations at the Rockefeller Foundation villa. The conference co-sponsors were represented by their agency heads. Others included McNamara, Salk and the heads or deputy heads of the Inter-American Development Bank (IDB), United States Agency for International Development (USAID), and of nine other international development agencies.

The few technical staff at that meeting included our Global Advisory Group (GAG) chair, Professor Kostrzewski; D. A. Henderson, now dean of the Johns Hopkins School of Hygiene and Public Health, and Bill Foege, director of the Centers for Disease Control and Prevention (CDC)—all enthusiastic EPI supporters. Sir Gustav Nossal, director of the Walter and Eliza Hall Institute of Medical Research, Australia, and Dr Ramalingaswami, director-general of the Indian Council of Medical Research (ICMR) might have been considered neutral, at least before hearing the Bellagio presentations. Philippe Stoeckel, and the minister and health director from Senegal were there for the Salk cause, the latter two really there only because of hosting the Mérieux-Dutch-sponsored studies. As there was only 'whisper' French translation, their participation was limited in any case.

If Salk's proposal had achieved some welcome outside of WHO when first made, by 1984 it was not viable. Salk still pushed the idea of using IPV with only two contacts per year to provide immunisations to children. Although we understood that under extreme conditions only two visits might be feasible, this made no sense for a general recommendation. Children had to be caught as quickly and as often as feasible after birth to get the vaccine schedule completed. A child born just after the six-monthly visit of a team would not get its first immunisation until six months later, and would remain unprotected until the second dose at a year of age. And we chose to use OPV based not only on its lower costs, but also on the fact that the viruses spread from those immunised to immunise other susceptibles in the community (but also having the drawback of, rarely, actually causing polio).

I led the presentations with two papers, outlining the burdens posed by vaccine-preventable diseases in developing countries and the state of our current immunisation efforts (now making good progress, thank you!) (see Figure 6.2).[5] I could report that 'The basic materials and methods are available for providing immunization...for all children of the World' (Bellagio Conference 1984: 18).

Sir Gus gave an update on vaccine research initiatives and DA presented a paper on childhood immunisation as an impetus to PHC. Bill talked about strategies and costs for expanding immunisation

FIGURE 6.2: Immunisation Coverage Estimates, 1974–83

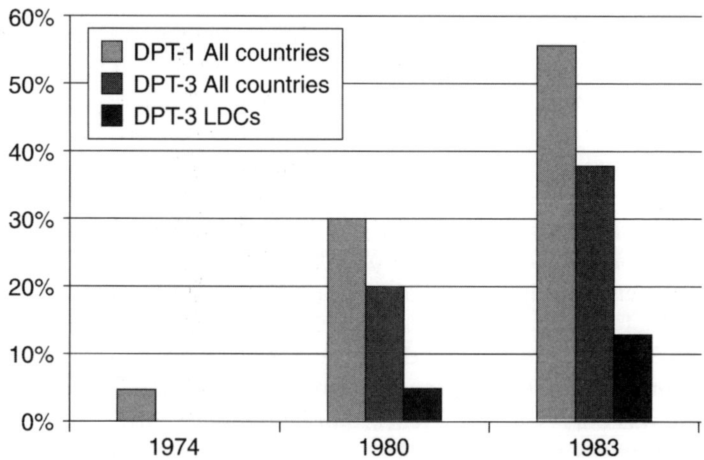

coverage in developing countries. He also referred to Grant's selected initiatives that would be facilitated by the infrastructure built by successful immunisation programmes. Oral rehydration therapy was given prominence as Peter McPherson, head of USAID, had now joined Grant as a vocal advocate.

Philippe Stoeckel presented the last paper on the agenda on the results of the trials using mobile teams to deliver vaccines at six-month intervals in Upper Volta, Senegal and Mali. Teams delivered BCG and a first dose of DPT and Salk polio vaccines at three to eight months of age, and measles, yellow fever and a second DPT and IPV dose at nine to fourteen months of age. Coverage results for 'target children' were reported only for Upper Volta and Senegal. In Upper Volta, 68 per cent coverage had been achieved in rural areas and 89 per cent in cities. The figures were 60 per cent and 40 per cent in Senegal. One dispensary in Senegal reported a polio decline, having seen only one case in an unimmunised child after the immunisation round.

To be fair, these rural areas posed heavy logistical challenges and fixed health facilities were not sufficient to provide any alternative. So, indeed, the strategy would be feasible and of lower cost. But it was not seriously considered as an alternative to the use of OPV and EPI's outreach strategy for covering women and children not regularly attending health facilities.

During the conference, the various luminaries and purse-controllers listened politely to the pitch we made for the $100 million that McNamara had suggested as our target. The amount was, indeed, a pittance in relation to the overall amounts provided in developmental assistance and there was plentiful evidence that immunisation programmes were among the most cost-effective within the health sector. The donors were not convinced, however. They did not see immunisation as a high priority or an investment in health as so essential for development. They suggested that countries simply take some of their current support and use it for immunisation. (Rational, but unrealistic, in part because developing countries themselves had yet to make immunisation a priority.)

Grant, Mahler, McNamara, Morse (head of UNDP) and Warren scrambled to bring a positive result from the proceedings. They agreed to create and to co-sponsor the 'Task Force for Child Survival'. It would act as a catalyst/coordinating body mainly in support of immunisation, but also including the other initiatives on the Grant GOBI-FFF list. Bill Foege was just stepping down from being the director, CDC, and he agreed to become executive director. This development not only saved face for the conference, it provided the solution to Grant and Mahler's 'red herring' problem. This was the mouse that emerged from McNamara's roar. It became a mighty mouse!

The Task Force for Child Survival

The Task Force for Child Survival was a remarkable creation, not the least because it was illegal. Well, at least in the eyes of our WHO lawyers! I spent many weeks in drafting and redrafting the 'Memoranda of Understanding', the normal basis for formalising cooperation among different UN agencies. None were acceptable. Our lawyers could not countenance including the Rockefeller Foundation, a private entity outside of the UN's purview, in the agreement. (No other agencies seemed to have problems, but I think this simply may have reflected benign neglect.) So we all just did without any formal agreement. The actions of our respective organisations were all voluntary in any case, the only real obligation being to pay a contribution of some $250,000 per biennium to provide for the secretariat.

That secretariat consisted of Bill Foege and two of his former CDC colleagues: Bill Watson, a former CDC deputy director and a legendary administrator, and Carol Walters, Watson's previous administrative assistant at CDC and a legend in her own right. (Bill took this same team to help the Carter Center recover from its troubled management when he became its executive director in 1986.) Consultants also joined for variable periods.

The Task Force organised and sponsored the succeeding 'Bellagio' meetings and served as their secretariat. Grant played a central role in identifying where to hold meetings and in using UNICEF resources to support the attendance of health ministers and other high-level participants from developing countries.

The Task Force functioned admirably as a neutral catalyst among these agencies. It had no authority to coordinate or to implement and did not compete with them for funding. It posed no threat, especially with Foege at the helm, who rivalled our GAG chair Kostrzewski in his use of diplomacy and humour. We met at least twice a year for one day, most often in New York City where three of the co-sponsors were headquartered.

Our meetings often started with a wide-ranging discussion on broad health matters, helped by data that the secretariat had summarised. And that led us to discuss how our individual organisations might help promote actions supporting immunisation as well as other aspects of child survival and development.

Each of us was frank about our own agency's shortcomings. I could complain, for example, about problems with our country staff that sometimes did too little, and UNICEF could talk about their country staff that sometimes did too much! We also had to see what might be done to reduce policy conflicts.

One related to ORS. Grant always seemed to be rushing into some sort of campaign, an enthusiasm that had been reinforced by successful immunisation days held in Colombia (described later). While I sometimes had reservations with the immunisation campaigns UNICEF sponsored elsewhere, I did not generally protest. When he proposed a campaign to promote ORS, however, all of us in the Task Force were dismayed. One achieves little by simply handing out ORS packets other than short-term publicity.

I cannot be certain that in this instance we caused his change of heart (he abandoned the notion), but I do know we strengthened the position of Steve Joseph, representing UNICEF on the Task Force, and his ability to argue his case with Grant. I will describe additional examples ahead. It is certainly the case that the regular face-to-face meetings at the Task Force prevented misunderstandings and facilitated my working with my UNICEF colleagues to preserve and strengthen our collaboration.

The Task Force's mode of operation—acting as a neutral catalyst among parties with divergent interests—very soon gained warm appreciation from the development community beyond the co-sponsors themselves. It secured domestic support after leaving the international scene temporarily in 1997 as a consequence of the co-sponsors ending their contributions. Its domestic efforts blossomed, however, and it was soon back again as a major player internationally. It is now the Task Force for Global Health. A mighty mouse, indeed!

I have mentioned Ilze's participation in meetings previously, and she often attended Task Force meetings with me as well. But it was not always easy for her. Under the label of 'wife', she was suspect. Wives have no place in meetings. This paragraph comes here because one of the most egregious incidents happened at the Rockefeller Foundation when Scott Halsted, our host, made her sit outside in the library rather than joining us. Space was not the issue, nor was confidentiality. It was simple prejudice. Even had she not been professionally trained as a pharmacist, nor had field experience with me doing surveys in Africa, her role of 'wife' should have gained her admission. As mere 'wife', she still worked hard for the EPI as hostess at home and as eyes and ears in receptions and meetings elsewhere. Not every wife has the time or interest to do what she did, but those who do deserve consideration.

NOTES

1. WHO/UNICEF, http://www.who.int/immunization/monitoring_surveillance/data/regions/en/.

2. The plan comprised the following:

(i) Promote the Expanded Program on Immunization (EPI) within the context of Primary Health Care.

(ii) Invest adequate human resources in EPI.

(iii) Invest adequate financial resources in EPI.

(iv) Ensure that programmes are continuously evaluated and adapted so as to achieve high immunisation coverage and maximum reduction in target-disease cases and deaths.

(v) Pursue research efforts as part of programme operations.

3. I have two anecdotes about Philippe, an engaging rogue with whom Ilze and I maintained warm relationships despite professional differences. Ilze attended many of the EPI meetings and we would often come to breakfast to join Philippe. He was very courteous and would rise with a slight bow in greeting. Unfortunately, he had somehow perfected the manoeuvre in such a way that when he sat back down, he sank the end of his tie into his coffee. We came to expect this! And I recall picking up the phone in my office one day to hear Philippe say: 'Hi Ralph. I'm here in Paris driving around in my car that has a phone.' Indeed, he was one of the first persons we knew to have one! I was laughing as I warmly congratulated him.

4. Email correspondence with W. H. Foege, dated 9 August 2012.

5. WHO/UNICEF, http://www.who.int/immunization/monitoring_surveillance/data/regions/en/.

7

'Bellagio' II–IV

A map without Utopia on it is not worth drawing.

Oscar Wilde

'Bellagio II', Cartagena, Colombia, October 1985

The number of Cartagena participants expanded almost as fast as immunisation coverage itself! They increased from 34 in Bellagio to 87. The first meeting was designed to raise funds from the donor community. The number of participants was small enough so substantial work got done, even though the result was disappointing. Subsequent meetings were promotional. They were designed as cheerleading events to encourage donors and developing countries alike to get on the immunisation bandwagon. Immunisation coverage was now about 67 per cent for a first dose of DPT, showing that services were being delivered. But the 50 per cent coverage for a third dose showed the problem of drop-out rates and, of course, the 19 per cent for a third dose in the least developed countries (LDCs) showing how much additional work was needed there (Figure 7.1).[1]

Grant's choice of Colombia was no accident. President Belisario Betancur Cuartas delivered the opening speech. He had created the national vaccination 'crusade' and had demonstrated what could be done when he led the country in mobilising all sectors of society in carrying out 'journados'—special days devoted to immunisation.

FIGURE 7.1: Immunisation Coverage Estimates, 1974–85

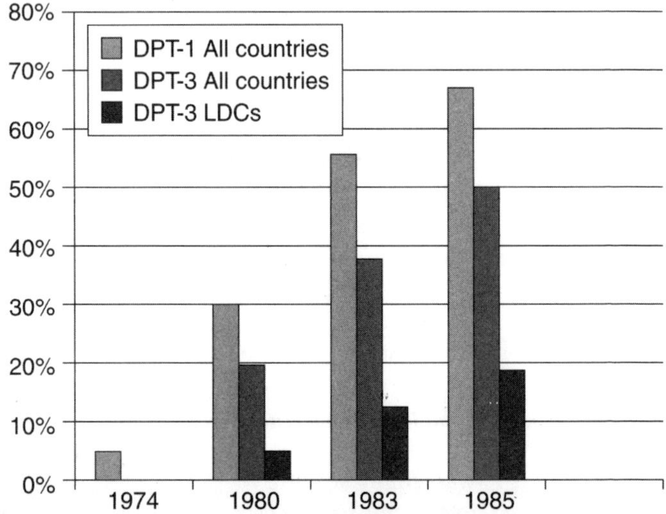

Teachers and the military were among those charged with getting children to immunisation sites. He said that Colombia has done '...in one year what in another way would have taken 5 years' (Task Force on Child Survival 1986: 11).

The Colombia story was inspirational. Grant was very impressed at how such days had been used so effectively in mobilising so many groups. He had, by then, invented the term Universal Childhood Immunization (UCI) that he could promote as a UNICEF initiative. He proclaimed this 'the leading edge' of the 'Child Survival Revolution' launched in 1983 with the first of *The State of the World's Children* reports by UNICEF. Of course this caused both annoyance within the WHO and general confusion for the staff of our two organisations. We all had to scramble to devise the explanation that UCI represented the immunisation goal, while the EPI was the programme through which the goal was to be achieved. (Whew!)

In any case, the Cartagena meeting was designed to focus on achieving UCI by 1990. Unlike our WHO language, which included reducing morbidity and mortality from our target diseases and which had envisioned immunising *all* children, UCI now specified reaching at least 80 per cent of children by that date.[2] Grant had his own reasons for the modifications: he had a sellable slogan and what he called a 'doable' goal for national leaders. This was something they could actually achieve if they tried.

'Accelerated' dominated 'expanded' throughout the meeting. Of course, we ourselves had started this in 1982 by having the World Health Assembly (WHA) issue its warning.[3] Yet, how would 'acceleration' differ from the old 'vertical' disease control campaigns and serve as a building block for other priority interventions and for primary health care (PHC) in general? As UNICEF cranked up the pressure for quick action, this compounded the 'red herrings' tensions and caused us many headaches.

We and our UNICEF counterparts went to work on drafting 'Planning principles for accelerated immunization activities' (WHO EPI and UNICEF 1985). It was a joint statement that attempted to rationalise how 'acceleration' fit within 'expansion' and within PHC as a whole. It emphasised acceleration by strengthening existing health services, but also recognised using the national immunisation days that UNICEF was emphasising. Helped by our Task Force exchanges, we were able to put some saving face on what in reality was quite a fundamental difference in philosophies.

Whatever the rhetoric, the stated WHO Expanded Programme on Immunization (EPI) strategy, not to mention the actual strategies being employed by national programmes, had certainly evolved markedly from that which Frank Schofield and colleagues had proclaimed as policy at the beginning: 'Immunization services will expand only as fast as the health services are expanded. The two are intrinsically linked.'[4] Now the focus was on supporting countries in what they could manage; more 'vertical' in those with less developed general health services, more 'horizontal' where the health services had broader reach. And reaching the 1990 goal now appeared actually feasible! And so on to the meeting in Talloires, France in 1988.

Talloires, France, March 1988: An Agenda for the 1990s

Although nowhere nearly as restricted as in Bellagio, housing was limited at the Tufts University Conference facilities in the small and scenic town of Talloires, and the participants numbered 60. Quality did not suffer, however! They included, in addition to the traditional

United Nations and donor agency heads and staff, the ministers of health from Brazil, China, Colombia, Morocco, Nigeria, Peru and Uganda, plus the vice-minister from Mexico. India, Pakistan and Indonesia were also represented.

The meeting had an inauspicious start. Talloires is within a couple of hours driving distance from Geneva. Bill Foege had stopped in Geneva and I drove him and a couple of others to the meeting. We left in plenty of time for Bill's opening speech before dinner. I was a little disconcerted to find that the battery in my BMW car (that had functioned perfectly up to then) was barely charged enough to start. But start it finally did and off we went.

As dusk was gathering, we reached the French frontier only to find traffic stopped. The frontier guards had gone on strike! I did not dare stop the car because of the low battery. To complicate matters, I also had a fuel problem as I had not started out with a full tank of gas. And what to do about Bill's speech?

Happily, the strike lasted only a little more than an hour and both the battery and the gas held out. Of course, no one carried cell phones then, so we could not warn anyone of our delay. When we finally did arrive, we found that all the talks had been postponed until after dinner, and the evening went off without a hitch.

Professor Kostrzewski chaired the next day's opening session that consisted of presentations by Bill on demographic trends, me on immunisation, Ciro de Quadros on polio eradication in the Americas, Mike Merson (director of the WHO Diarrhoeal Diseases Control Program) on control of these diseases (including the use of ORS) and, finally, a presentation by Fred Sai (former minister of health of Ghana) on the role of family planning in child survival and development. This set the table for the following presentations and panel discussions which focused on reactions from ministers of health or their representatives, from Rotary International and from the major international development agencies.

Coverage continued upward, DPT-3 at some 56 per cent in 1987 (Figure 7.2).[5] The LDCs still lagged at 29 per cent. Yet the delivery infrastructure was building rapidly.

Grant was determined by this stage that 'UCI by 1990' would be achieved, even if we missed by a bit. After all, the progress had really been spectacular and it was now time to celebrate success and move on to other important issues. Grant had his attention fixed on his next big event: the World Summit for Children. He planned this for

FIGURE 7.2: Immunisation Coverage Estimates, 1974–87

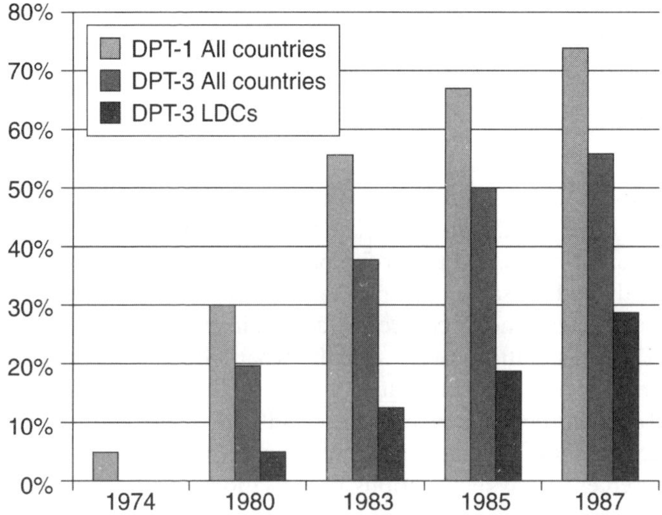

September 1990 at the UN, the date chosen was close to the General Assembly, thereby allowing the attendance of as many heads of state as possible.

Polio posed an interesting dilemma. In 1985, the Pan American Health Organization (PAHO) Directing Council unanimously passed a resolution calling for the eradication of wild poliovirus in the Americas. By the time of the Talloires meeting, Ciro de Quadros, who was mainly responsible for getting this resolution passed, was convinced this had already been achieved and was anxious that a similar goal now be set globally. We at headquarters were not confident of that achievement. I wanted to wait until we were sure before going for global eradication.

But just previously, in January 1988, Dr Hiroshi Nakajima, then the director of the WHO Regional Office for the Western Pacific, had been nominated by the WHO Executive Board to replace Dr Mahler as director-general that July. There were many questions about Dr Nakajima, not the least of which was his willingness to support polio eradication. So Grant approached Mahler to see whether WHO could endorse eradication before Nakajima took over. Mahler asked me, and I indicated my reasons for wanting a delay, but, under the circumstances, I agreed to support global eradication now.

The Talloires participants were upbeat about our reports, despite the cold and rainy weather. The overall news was good. But then we pulled somewhat of a fast one on them. In preparation for Talloires, I had worked with our other WHO programmes to put together targets to be achieved by the year 2000. These included the virtual elimination of neonatal tetanus, a 90 per cent reduction in measles cases and a 95 per cent reduction in measles deaths, a 70 per cent reduction in under-5 deaths due to diarrhoea, a 25 per cent reduction in under-5 case/fatality rates associated with acute respiratory infection, reduction of infant and under-5 mortality rates in all countries by at least half, and the same reduction in all countries of current maternal mortality rates. And of course I added polio eradication as well.

These aspirations were exactly what Grant wanted to have endorsed at the summit. But it was clear that the participants of the Talloires meeting, even if they had had a personal inclination to support these (and some did not), could not act without formal endorsement from their various organisations. And there certainly was no time for that!

So the Task Force itself, an ad hoc group with no formal standing, issued the 'Declaration of Talloires'. It listed these targets and urged national governments and the international community to mobilise the resources and conduct the research needed to attain them. The participants heard the declaration read and there were no outraged demands to reject it, but that is not quite the same as formal approval. That made little difference, however, as the way in which the declaration was publicised and used certainly gave the impression of approval.

And it did its job. This was the first time to my knowledge that such a set of development targets had been put in a document purporting to represent a consensus of the international health community.

Bangkok, Thailand, March 1990: A Call for Action

This would prove to be the last of the 'Bellagio' meetings, at least in part because much of what had been originally envisioned in the first meeting concerning immunisation had been achieved. DPT-3 was now about 75 per cent, 55 per cent in the LDCs (Figure 7.3).[6] (In later years, global coverage would falter, mainly reflecting loss of UNICEF support. Subsequently, with the formation of the Global Alliance for Vaccines and Immunization [GAVI] in 2000, coverage began a sustained path of increase with GAVI now adding new vaccines as they became available.)

FIGURE 7.3: Immunisation Coverage Estimates, 1974–2010

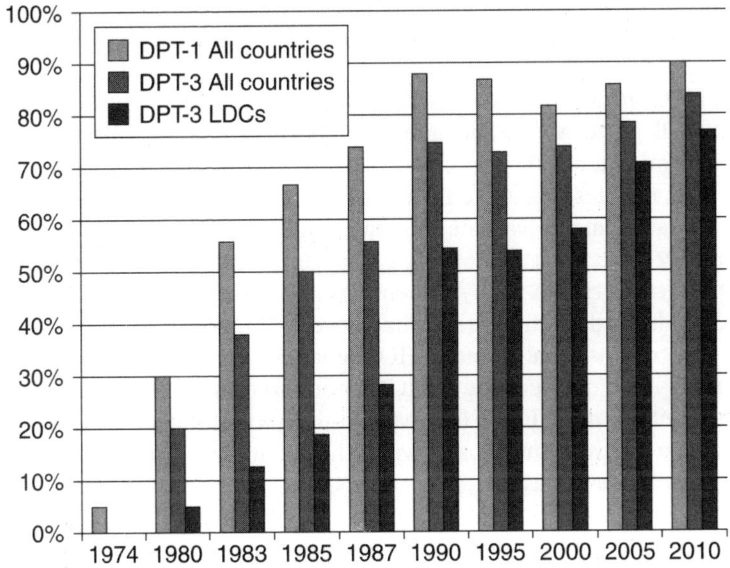

There were 107 listed participants at that meeting. Dr Nakajima was now WHO director-general and I was one of the assistant directors-general. The agenda, while still emphasising immunisation, was broadened to allow the formation of working groups that discussed child survival and development goals, women's health, research, and 'weaving the fabric of health' relating to how these specific areas related to PHC as a whole.

Continuing the ploy introduced in Talloires, the Task Force issued the 'Affirmation of Bangkok' that now included affirming 'the desirability and feasibility of attaining the WHO/UNICEF Common Goals for the Health of Women and Children by the year 2000'. These goals had been expanded since Talloires and were now grouped under the rubrics of reduction in mortality, women's education and health, better nutrition, control of childhood diseases and control of the environment. They would find their way into the 'Goals for Children and Development in the 1990s' that were appended to the Declaration and Plan of Action from the World Summit for Children that took place that September. That, in turn, was a further step in their evolution to become incorporated within the health component of the 'Millennium Development Goals'.[7]

Dr Nakajima, representing WHO as a co-sponsor, made gracious and complimentary remarks about the meeting and about the Task Force. But, in fact, he was a reluctant participant. He was extremely jealous of WHO prerogatives and primacy of place. The WHO constitution, after all, states that one of the functions of WHO '...shall be to act as the directing and coordinating authority on international health work...'

In my presentation to the meeting, I had suggested the usefulness of establishing a 'vaccine purchase fund'. (GAVI now does this.) But Dr Nakajima took strong exception to the idea. He took even stronger exception to my presenting it without clearing it first with him, although such clearance had never been requested and was not by any means usual within WHO. He said that I was a half-time CDC employee, a quarter-time UNICEF employee, and only quarter-time committed to WHO. (I felt that full-time commitment to WHO in fact entailed working closely with others, but Nakajima was not of a collaborative mindset.)

Nakajima's criticism of me was pretty typical of his behaviour in general. He felt that he had to disparage his senior staff and he would often challenge me by saying incredulously: 'You don't know this?' He not only had a mind like flypaper in remembering details, he had special Japanese staff he used as encyclopaedias, sending them off to chase information. He preferred them to regular WHO staff that might tattle about where he had acquired his knowledge.

In any case, nothing came of my suggestion then. The World Bank and others indicated there was no place for any additional international financing facility or mechanism. And although I think Dr Nakajima never changed his views on my loyalties, it posed few practical problems for me.

There were two additional meetings that carried on the 'Bellagio' tradition with the Task Force (now named the 'Task Force for Child Survival and Development') acting as secretariat. 'Ending Hidden Hunger', focusing on micronutrients, was held in Montreal in October

1991, following the World Summit for Children. The Canadian International Development Agency and the United States Agency for International Development (USAID) added their names to WHO, UNICEF, the World Bank and United Nations Development Programme (UNDP), along with the Food and Agriculture Organization (FAO). The Rockefeller Foundation dropped out. The meeting report contained position papers and summarised discussions held in workshops, but issued no declaration.

The Bellagio co-sponsors joined for their final meeting on 'Achieving Health' in New Delhi, India, in February 1994. While promoting integrated services, participants also emphasised achieving the set of mid-decade health goals that had their origins in Talloires and had now been jointly endorsed by WHO and UNICEF. Jim Grant would die the following January and with him, the driving force for these international promotional meetings. His replacement as UNICEF executive-director, Carol Bellamy, chose not to continue his championship of immunisation.

Notes

1. WHO/UNICEF, http://www.who.int/immunization/monitoring_surveillance/data/regions/en/.

2. Task Force on Child Survival (1986). Grant's remarks to the conference participants actually state 'to actually achieve by 1990 virtual universal child immunization, with levels of protection of 80% to 85% within a country.'

3. Thirty-fifth World Health Assembly, resolution WHA35.31, 14 May 1982.

4. Printed but unpublished and undated booklet, presumably issued in 1974 or 1975, entitled *World Health Organization: WHO Expanded Programme on Immunization.*

5. WHO/UNICEF, http://www.who.int/immunization/monitoring_surveillance/data/regions/en/.

6. WHO/UNICEF, http://www.who.int/immunization/monitoring_surveillance/data/regions/en/.

7. See http://www.unmillenniumproject.org/goals/. The Millennium Development Goals (MDGs) are eight international development goals that were officially established following the Millennium Summit of the United Nations in 2000, following the adoption of the United Nations

Millennium Declaration. All 193 United Nations Member States and at least 23 international organisations agreed to achieve these goals by the year 2015. The goals are:

(i) Eradicating extreme poverty and hunger
(ii) Achieving universal primary education
(iii) Promoting gender equality and empowering women
(iv) Reducing child mortality rates
(v) Improving maternal health,
(vi) Combating HIV/AIDS, malaria, and other diseases
(vii) Ensuring environmental sustainability
(viii) Developing a global partnership for development

Part 4

Over and Out

8

Transitions

It's a sin to speak ill of others, but it's seldom a mistake.

Oscar Wilde

Moving Up

After his confirmation as director-general in July 1988, Dr Nakajima proposed making me assistant director-general (ADG) on the retirement in late 1989 of the 'American' ADG, Warren Furth. (I put the nationality in quotes because international civil servants, as we all were, are not supposed to exhibit any favouritism towards their home countries.) I did not welcome the 'promotion'. A joke circulated within the World Health Organization that told of an auction of brains, including that of Einstein. An ADG brain was valued over all others as it had never been used. I had suggested to Dr Nakajima the names of several other Americans whom I thought would be preferable, but he could not be dissuaded. A colleague said to me: 'The air is higher, but thinner.' I was definitely paying back WHO for the opportunity I had been given to direct the Expanded Program on Immunization.

Dr Nakajima wanted to cushion the influence of the United States in WHO's financial management. Warren Furth had been in charge of administration throughout the Mahler years and Americans before him had traditionally held this post, just as the 'Russian' ADG traditionally held the responsibility for communicable diseases.

I was the bait for the swap he negotiated. He would make me the communicable disease ADG if the US would agree that a Brit would take over administration. It was agreed. A new 'Russian' ADG then acquired the portfolio that included environmental issues, chronic diseases, occupational health and the promotion of healthy lifestyles.

Ko (Jacobus) Keja and I discussed what to do about a new EPI director. Ko was to retire the next year (1989), so he was not a candidate. Ciro de Quadros certainly was, as was Bob Kim-Farley (EIS class of 1981), at that time working as EPI advisor in the South-East Asia Regional Office. Ko strongly supported Bob, who had excellent technical skills and was a hard worker. We were warned that his management skills might be a bit weak, but Ko expected to stay on after retirement as a consultant to help him. He thought that Ciro's 'go for the jugular' management style would alienate the regional offices.

Dr Nakajima accepted our recommendation of Bob, who joined us in 1989 as medical officer and would be director of EPI by 1990. But Ko was absent: he had died in his sleep from a massive heart attack just following retirement. Bob had difficulties and in 1994 it was decided to replace him. He returned to Southeast Asia and performed well in assignments that included being the WHO representative for India and then Indonesia.

On Bob's departure, the question of succession again arose. Dr Nakajima had a very favourable view of Ciro, who was an extremely effective manager. He came to Geneva to look the situation over. Naturally enough, he supposed that I had been the one principally opposed to his replacing me. While this was not the case, he had reason to think so.

We had clashed unpleasantly in his home over my informing one of his staff that there was a position open in another region he might be interested in. Ciro was furious. He certainly wanted the person to succeed and felt he was grooming him for advancement. But he wanted no interference from me or anyone else. This was a matter of principle on which we strongly disagreed, as, from my own experience under CDC director David Sencer, I thought everyone should be fully informed of the opportunities available.

So when Ciro came to Geneva, although I told him I would support him as EPI director, he dealt directly with Dr Nakajima and the various people and entities he was considering reorganising. He soon proposed that the EPI be included within a new entity:

the Global Program for Vaccines and Immunization (GPV). This would include the WHO Biologicals unit and the Children's Vaccine Initiative, a co-sponsored entity focused on research to improve vaccines.

He was not shy in telling staff what he proposed to do; James Cheyne being one of those told his services would no longer be needed! I was told he also proposed heading this new entity as ADG. In the event, however, Ciro, a Brazilian national, discovered that if he took the Geneva position he would lose his residency privileges in the US. He withdrew his candidacy. But his reorganisation proposal was endorsed by Dr Nakajima, although he balked at making its head an ADG.

With Ciro no longer a candidate, I went through several weeks of song and dance with Dr Nakajima in proposing Marc LaForce. Marc was a close personal friend, but no professional slouch! He had been a year behind me at both the Boston City Hospital and the Centers for Disease Control and Prevention/Epidemic Intelligence Service. He had done long-term consultancies for us in 1978–79 and 1985 and had made major contributions to our early development.[1] Dr Nakajima never said 'no', but, on the other hand, he never said 'yes' either!

Rumour had it that both Ciro and D. A. Henderson had made it known that they opposed Marc. In any case, Dr Nakajima had his own candidate, Jong Wook Lee. 'JW' was the EPI advisor in the regional office for the Western Pacific. But he also served as a principle advisor to the regional director and fellow Korean, Dr San Tae Han, who had succeeded Dr Nakajima to that position. JW had been active in managing Dr Han's successful efforts to become re-elected in 1994. He had done Han's bidding in obtaining votes, a dirty underbelly of WHO politics. It was too much. He wanted out and appealed to Dr Nakajima for a transfer. He was appointed director of the newly constituted GPV.

JW was both competent and extremely personable, himself becoming WHO director-general in 2002 (but dying, probably from a burst cranial aneurism, in 2006). I mentioned to him at our first meeting that I had preferred Marc as director, but would support him and the GPV as best I could. We became good friends and he was a first-class director. He did often fall asleep in my staff meetings, perhaps all too understandable, but also a symptom of the work he frequently did late into the night.

One consequence of Ko's death in 1989 was that polio eradication moved off from the EPI more quickly than might otherwise have happened. Ko kept doors open and was opposed to a split. But those doors closed when Bob arrived. The two medical officers working on polio were eager to embrace the mass polio immunisation days that had proved so successful in the Americas. By the time JW arrived, they pretty much operated on their own. It is the case that the loss of support for immunisation after 1990 doomed routine services in countries such as Bangladesh, where it was only the mass immunisation days that sustained services at all. So circumstances reinforced their preferences.

ADG Life in the Time of Nakajima

Each ADG office had two support staff: an administrative assistant and a secretary. Traditionally, these have been senior staff that can pretty much run the office on their own, and did so in many of these offices.

'Our' two support staff had served in the office of the 'Russian' AD'sG since long before my arrival. They were both from the United Kingdom (UK) and married to Italians (seemingly a preferred nationality for many of the UK secretaries coming to Geneva). As with all the ADG staff, they were the keepers of tradition and sticklers for error-free correspondence, and our two not infrequently drove our very busy secretarial staff to tears with their nitpicking. The resentment was intensified because the pace of the ADG office was leisurely, to say the least, and the ADG concerned could be expected to be served tea or coffee at his (there were no women) pleasure.

Our two knew all the communicable disease programmes and their various idiosyncrasies well. They had given me a warm welcome when I first came to their office in December 1976 for an introduction, helping me snag a very desirable, rent-controlled apartment within walking distance of WHO. Despite the frictions with my staff, we remained on friendly terms and they, quite naturally, assumed they would stay on with me.

But I decided to change. And though this was hard on them, they accepted the change with grace and moved over to serve the new

'Russian' ADG and so at least were able to continue that tradition. But this led me to the problem of having to choose my own staff!

Anyone who has done such choosing knows the hazards. I have been fooled by the esteem expressed by applicants for me or the programme and by the endorsements from supervisors. Foege, in his book *House on Fire*, has helpful suggestions, one being to have candidates home for a dinner or other informal event, another being to turn to co-workers and subordinates rather than supervisors (Foege 2011: 138–39). But even after exercising 'due diligence', the 'Peter Principle' may come into play: rising in bureaucracies to one's level of incompetence (Peter and Hull 1969). A person performing well at one level or at one sort of job may fail miserably placed somewhere else. But choose you must, hoping for the best.

I chose as administrative assistant a Swiss national who had worked at one time in the legal department and most recently for the Tropical Diseases Research and Training Program (TDR). She suggested for secretary a close and long-time friend, also Swiss, who was also working then for TDR. I followed her advice. Good idea! They were both terrific. Unlike the previous two, they had long experience 'in the trenches' and were known and respected by their colleagues within the various divisions. And they reciprocated by dealing with the division staff with respect and understanding of their constraints. Their good work made for an excellent office atmosphere and made up for many of the other drawbacks of being an ADG. (I got my own coffee, but they did help serve at staff meetings.)

I supervised the EPI, the Diarrhoeal Diseases Control Program, the Communicable Diseases and Tropical Diseases Divisions, and TDR (co-sponsored with the World Bank and the United Nations Development Programme). I tried to act as a buffer between them and Dr Nakajima, with varying success. Among my more memorable activities was acting as secretary for the 1992 Ministerial Conference on Malaria held in Amsterdam, coordinating the response from headquarters to the 1974 outbreak of plague in Surat, India, and playing a similar role in the 1995 outbreak of Ebola in Kikwit, Zaire. I could certainly have been busier had I chosen to take an active role in the divisions I supervised. I refrained, however. I had valued the benign neglect I had enjoyed in the EPI and felt my role was to do everything possible to help the directors with problems, not to try to run their programmes for them. But it was frustrating!

Out of the Frying Pan

A limit of two five-year terms was in effect when Dr Nakajima took office and he was obliged to retire in 1998. He was not an easy person to work under! But, although he was quick to criticise, he did not generally interfere with operations. His public image was poor. Although he could express himself clearly when he chose to, many of his public utterances puzzled audiences and his short stature, his 'comb-over' efforts to hide his baldness and his blindness in one eye did not enhance his physical appearance. Most damning, he was perceived as being corrupt. Perhaps the most publicised incident occurred in 1992 when he was accused in the Russian papers of trying to smuggle out six valuable icons (Altman 1992). So there was general relief when Gro Harlem Brundtland, former prime minister of Norway, replaced him in July 1998.

One of her first moves, understandable from her perspective, was to throw out Dr Nakajima's ADsG, retaining only Denis Aitken (the Brit) for administration. She really wanted a clean sweep. She needed Denis for the transition and he was extremely good at his job. I could understand her decision to replace me with a younger American, David Heymann, also of CDC/EIS heritage, who had experience in both the field and headquarters.

Brundtland permitted each of us 'old' ADsG the choice of leaving immediately or staying on if they were close to the standard UN retirement age of 62. (Prior to Dr Brundtland, this had not been enforced for ADsG.) I chose to stay, as I would retire in eight months (March 1999). I kept busy by helping with various chores and responsibilities as they emerged (including being acting director of the leprosy programme for a time). The only assignment I categorically refused was to go to New York City to become the WHO representative to the UN. The job involved endless bureaucracy and periodic babysitting the director-general when she visited. I told her principal advisor, Jonas Støre, that I had not come to WHO to do that! Ilze and I returned to Atlanta in October 1999.

Dr Brundtland did 'make a difference', a phrase she often used. She decided to reorganise WHO, a move that was generally seen as being long overdue. Scuttlebutt had it that this was Jonas Støre's idea and further that he followed, step by step, the prescription contained in *Leading Change*, a popular management book at the time (Kotter 1996). Whatever its other merits, however, each ADG was given wide latitude in creating his or her own administrative rules for what were now termed 'clusters'. This created internal chaos with conflicts and contradictions in procedures.

The situation was not improved when Dr Brundtland decided not to continue for a second term, leaving a mess for her successor. This was J. W. Lee, who began his term in 2003. The Korean government had come to an understanding with Norway before Dr Brundtland's election that they would defer supporting JW if she would make him a member of her staff, positioning him for her post when she vacated it.

Young Professionals—Not!

One task I did take on for Dr Brundtland while waiting for retirement was to establish a WHO programme for young professionals. I think she let me do this just to keep me out of mischief. The Scandinavian countries had, in Mahler's time, often sent their young professionals to individual WHO programmes for two-year assignments. But these ad hoc arrangements were not a cohesive programme and they became so unsatisfactory that the assignments stopped under Dr Nakajima.

I longed to create a programme similar to the EIS with its emphasis on practical working experiences under the close supervision of a competent supervisor. The young professionals trained each year by CDC constitute a pool of candidates for longer-term posts, either at CDC itself or for openings in state or local health departments. They are a prize institutional resource, both during the actual time of their training, when they perform essential duties, and when that training has ended. They would be a similar resource for WHO.

I had tried previously. The first effort, made shortly after I joined WHO in 1977, used our own funds to bring two young physicians from developing countries into WHO for two years, one serving in the Pan American Health Organization (PAHO) and one with us at headquarters. But we could not afford it; we needed those funds for other purposes. In the mid-1980s I tried again, bringing Jeff Koplan (who would later become director, CDC) from CDC to help me make a proposal that would receive adequate support. It was rejected by Dr Cohen, Dr Mahler's main advisor. He felt WHO was not a place to train; schools of public health should do that.

Dr Brundtland had received some undesignated funds from the Rockefeller Foundation to help her in her new position (a suggestion from Foege, it turns out).[2] She let me use some of them for the young professionals. I was able to get additional support from the UN Foundation of Ted Turner (of CNN and other fame) and was able to get CDC to second a staff member to manage the programme. A first class began in July 1999 after my departure from WHO. They suffered. I had not been able to raise sufficient funding, in part because no one within WHO thought these individuals should be paid at the professional grade. So they were not appointed as 'associate professionals' as the former young professionals had been. They were greeted as some sort of odd trainees. And no additional efforts were made to secure funding. The programme died with the first class.

I did not give up, however! I discussed the idea with JW during a visit he made to Atlanta in March 2003, when he had been nominated, but not yet confirmed, as director-general. He invited me to participate in a meeting in Bellagio, Italy, later that month where I made a presentation to him and others developing transition plans. He seemed seriously committed and I returned with Ilze at the end of June to spend two blazingly hot weeks in Geneva working on the proposal as a member of his transition team. From this emerged the broad outlines of the 'Health Leadership Service' (HLS).

This time our trainees would be 'officers' with full staff pay and privileges, similar to the model of the EIS. We had adequate start-up funding from the Bill and Melinda Gates Foundation, among others, and we could afford a rigorous two years of training and supervision. As a condition of receiving outside funds, WHO was obliged to begin providing support from its own budget after the first two years. JW arranged for me to return to Geneva at intervals during the following couple of years to help get it started. We were off and running!

Well, we were certainly off. But running? Not so much! The following were among our problems:

- JW did not want the programme housed in his office. Dave Sencer, former CDC director, told me that it could not work otherwise, but JW remained adamant.
- As could be expected, there was resentment in my returning as an agent of JW to actively promote the programme.

- I was to find out that the very competent and highly committed epidemiologist I selected to direct the HLS was also active in the staff association. In fact, she was more or less at war with most levels of the administration whose goodwill we sorely needed.
- The ADG to which the HLS was relegated had no appreciation for the merits of an EIS-like programme that was based on on-the-job mentoring rather than a programme leading to an academic degree. Our case was not helped by the administrator for this 'cluster', an American lady with whom I had clashed as ADG. She had little tolerance for flexibility or innovation. She was seethingly hostile to our efforts.
- There was scepticism that it was appropriate for us to train participants for work in WHO and other organisations engaged in health development work; training was for health workers within countries.
- The ADG in charge of administration was himself promoting a training initiative for current WHO staff and saw the HLS as expensive (as it was compared to other training schemes if run on WHO resources alone) and unnecessary.
- JW himself had other fish to fry and failed to provide the support needed to counter the hostility at the lower administrative levels.
- And, finally, I have myself to blame. I detest confrontation and avoided challenging JW and the two principal AD'sG in opposition, satisfying myself from the assurances JW always readily gave me that he would take care of the problems. They devolved instead on the epidemiologist-coordinator and her young administrator. She became so stressed and ill that she very nearly resigned from WHO.

We did try! Against many odds, a first class of HLS officers was trained and sent to field assignments under competent supervisors. But JW did not uphold WHO's end of the bargain to begin contributing after the start-up period. This refusal ended the adventure. This was 'pound wise and penny foolish'. I had good reason to believe that if WHO would support five officers, our proposal at the time, the donor community (especially the Scandinavian countries) would be prepared to restart sending their young professionals to join the HLS at no cost to WHO. This would have provided WHO with at least another five officers who would, of course, be trained, but who would be at the same time providing valuable professional services to the WHO. The failure of the HLS is a shame. WHO has so much to offer.

What Goes Around...

There were no more Geneva adventures in store for me after the demise of the HLS. But I keep a finger or two in the health pie. At CDC I participate in the 'Tuesday Morning Seminars' at which current classes of EIS officers present the results of investigations. I have also been a member of an advisory group providing oversight to a grant from the Bill and Melinda Gates Foundation supporting research related to the elimination or control of 'neglected tropical diseases'.[3] This is coordinated by an Atlanta secretariat housed in the Task Force for Global Health, the current metamorphosis of the original Task Force for Child Survival.

Harking back to the EPI, my principal role in that advisory group has been to keep an eye on monitoring and evaluation activities that include both coverage surveys and surveillance activities to look for continuing transmission or recurrence of the target diseases. I have even applied an EPI-like cluster survey design to look at the prevalence in *Culex* mosquitoes of the microscopic larva through which they transmit lymphatic filariasis. It may prove a sensitive approach for detecting ongoing transmission in humans.

Final Reflections

One is generally expected to end a memoir such as this with grand insights on the WHO, the state of 'Global Health' and the world in general. I know Richard Feynman warned against the temptation of persons who have succeeded in one area then believing they have legitimacy in pronouncing on unrelated issues. (I always thought Jonas Salk succumbed to this.) I have few illusions about the possibility of my saying anything new, even within the narrow domains in which I have worked. I hope that by simply telling what happened, people can draw their own conclusions.

And yet...!

- It has been a grand adventure. It was an extraordinary privilege to serve in the WHO, whether in good times or bad. Join it if you have the opportunity. You will meet colleagues of extraordinary ability and commitment. You will learn a lot!
- While I wish it were a more effective institution in general, WHO is not likely to change. Try for change, surely, but get to work to help it support countries to address their health problems.
- Health workers in the developing world succeed under conditions that most of us from privileged environments could not tolerate. They are unsung heroes and heroines. Empathise with them and support them.
- Apply what we already know. Acquiring new knowledge is important, but knowledge of any sort is not useful unless applied. And it is not being fully applied.
- International health development is messy and there are many failures. Corruption, political instability and violence complicate life. That is no excuse for not acting. There are major success stories, especially in controlling infectious diseases, in lowering infant mortality, in decreasing birth rates and in increasing longevity. All this contributes to the economic growth that most developing countries are experiencing. That development is essential for our future.

That should do it.

NOTES

1. Email correspondence with LaForce, dated 28 June 2013. His career hardly suffered! During the 1990s, he advised the polio programme and chaired a Steering Committee on Epidemiology and Field Research for the Global Program on Vaccines (of which the EPI was then a part). During the 2000 decade, he led the Meningitis Vaccine Project, resulting in the development, production and delivery of a highly effective vaccine against meningococcus A, the strain responsible for the epidemics that have devastated the 'meningococcal belt' of Africa. He received the Albert B. Sabin award for this in 2012.

2. Email correspondence with W. H. Foege, dated June 2014.

3. The number of these diseases varies with each advocacy group, but in this case they are limited to lymphatic filariasis, onchocerciasis,

schistosomiasis, soil transmitted helminthes and trachoma. These are all problems for impoverished populations in the topics and they are all being currently addressed by providing medications, for the most part donated by the major pharmaceutical companies, on a once or twice-yearly schedule.

References

Altman, L. K. 1992. 'Head of U.N. Health Agency is Embroiled in Battle for Re-election.' *The New York Times*, 10 August.

Bellagio Conference. 1984. *Protecting the World's Children: Vaccines and Immunization within Primary Health Care*. A Bellagio Conference, 13–15 March. New York: The Rockefeller Foundation.

Bennett, B. et al. 1994. 'A Computer Simulation of Household Sampling Schemes for Health Surveys in Developing Countries'. *International Journal of Epidemiology* 23(8): 1282–91.

Dave, K. H. 1983. 'Measles in India'. *Reviews of Infectious Diseases* http://www.ncbi.nlm.nih.gov/pubmed/6878990 5(3): 406–10.

Foege, W. H. 2011. *House on Fire*. University of California Press, Milbank Memorial Fund.

Henderson, R. H. and T. Sunderasan. 1982. 'Cluster Sampling to Assess Immunization Coverage: A Review of Experience with a Simplified Sampling Method'. *Bulletin of the World Health Organization* 60(2): 253–60.

Henderson, R. H., and M. Yekpe. 1969. 'Smallpox Transmission in Southern Dahomey. A Study of a Village Outbreak'. *American Journal of Epidemiology* 90(5): 423–28.

Henderson, R. H., H. Davis, D. L. Eddins, and W. H. Foege. 1973. 'Assessment of Vaccination Coverage, Vaccination Scar Rates and Smallpox Scarring in Five Areas of West Africa'. *Bulletin of the World Health Organization* 48: 183–94.

Kotter, J. P. 1996. *Leading Change*. Boston, Massachusetts: Harvard Business School Press.

Lemeshow, S., A. G. TserKovnyi, J. L. Tulloch, S. K. Lwanga, and J. Keja. 1985. 'A Computer Simulation of the EPI Survey Strategy'. *International Journal of Epidemiology* 14(3): 473–81.

Lumen, E. T., M. Sabian, S. Stokley, M. M. McCauley, and K. M. Shaw. 2008. 'Impact of Methodological "Shortcuts" in Conducting Public Health Surveys: Results from a Vaccination Coverage Survey'. *BMC Public Health* 8.

Machiavelli, Niccolo. 1909–14. *The Prince* (N. H. Thomson, trans.), Vol. XXXVI, Part 1, The Harvard Classics. New York: P. F. Collier & Son.

Melnick, J. L. 1982. 'Advantages and Disadvantages of Killed and Live Poliomyelitis Vaccines'. *Bulletin of the World Health Organization* 56(1): 21–38.

Meyer, H. M., et al. 1964. 'Response of Volta Children to Live Attenuated Measles Virus Vaccine'. *Bulletin of the World Health Organization* 30(6): 769–81.

Milligan, P., N. Alpha and S. Bennett. 2003. 'Comparisons of Two Cluster Sampling Methods for Health Surveys in Developing Countries'. *International Journal of Epidemiology* 33(3): 469–76.

Nicholas, D. D., J. H. Kratzer, S. Ofosu-Amaah, and D. W. Belcher. 1977. 'Outside Europe. Is Poliomyelitis a Serious Problem in Developing Countries?–The Danfa Experience'. *British Medical Journal* 1(6067): 1009–12.

Ofosu-Amaah, S., J. H. Kratzer, and D. D. Nicholas. 1977. 'Is Poliomyelitis a Serious Problem in Developing Countries? – Lameness in Ghanaian Schools'. *British Medical Journal* 1(6067): 1012–14.

Peter, L. J. and Raymond Hull. 1969. *The Peter Principle: Why Things Always go Wrong*. New York: William Morrow.

Serfling, R. E. and I. L. Sherman. 1965. 'Attribute Sampling Methods for Local Health Departments: With Special Reference to Immunization Surveys'. US Public Health Service publication no. 1230, Washington, D.C., US GPO.

Task Force on Child Survival. 1986. *Protecting the World's Children: "Bellagio II" at Cartagena, Colombia, October 1985*, Rockefeller Foundation conference report. Decatur, Georgia: The Task Force for Child Survival and Rockefeller Foundation.

United Nations Children's Fund (UNICEF). 1982. *The State of the World's Children*. New York: Oxford University Press (for UNICEF).

Walsh, J. A., and K. W. Warren. 1979. 'Selective Primary Health Care: An Interim Strategy for Disease Control in Developing Countries'. *New England Journal of Medicine* 301(18): 967–74.

WHO Expanded Programme on Immunization (EPI) and UNICEF. 1985. *Planning Principles for Accelerated Immunization Activities: A Joint WHO/UNICEF Statement*. Geneva: World Health Organization.

Index